WHAT ABOUT US?

WHAT ABOUT US?

AN OPEN LETTER TO THE MOTHERS
FEMINISM FORGOT

MAUREEN FREELY

BLOOMSBURY

First Published 1995

Copyright © 1995 by Maureen Freely

The moral right of the author has been asserted

Bloomsbury Publishing Plc, 2 Soho Square, London W1V 6HB

A CIP catalogue record for this book is available
from the British Library

ISBN 0 7475 23045

Typeset by Hewer Text Composition Services, Edinburgh
Printed in Great Britain by Clays Ltd, St Ives plc

Acknowledgements

I owe thanks and apologies to Frank Longstreth, Paul Spike, Liz Calder, Mary Tomlinson, Maggie Traugott, Joseph Olshan, Cecilia Pyper, Alexandra Pringle, Nicci Gerrard, Lynn Bryden, Tom McCaskie, Polly Spearman, Nicky Sparkes and Jane Lopez, not to mention Matthew, Emma, Kimber, Rachel, Helen, and – last but not least – Pandora.

Dedication

In memory of Mary Ellmann, whose book, *Thinking About Women*, made me think again about mothers by first making me laugh.

Contents

Preface

When the second wave of feminism began in the late sixties, its most ardent rallying cry was that a woman had the right to shape her own destiny. Not only was it wrong to be coerced into motherhood: it was also wrong to have to give up work in order to have children – or go without them in order to work. No more Hobson's choices, we said, no more women stuck in ruts. From now on we were going to work together to find new ways of bringing mothers into the mainstream.

How have we fared?

As the public record shows, not as brilliantly as hoped. There's been trouble getting maternity leave, trouble getting flexible working hours, trouble getting adequate childcare, trouble getting men to do more than forty-one minutes of housework a year. Or is it forty-seven? It's common knowledge that working mothers face a double shift, but despite this unappetising threat, the record also shows that more and more of us are prepared to take it on. We are the foot soldiers Susan Faludi salutes as we plod along the wrong side of the indistinct horizon. We are the living statistics who prove that feminism is still going strong in spite of, in defiance of, the anti-feminist backlash.

Yes, but how do *we* feel about what we've been through? Having been through it, how do we feel about feminism? What has it been like to belong to a generation of warrior guinea-pigs? What's our verdict now on the generation that preceded us, the great feminist thinkers who gave us our ideas and our walking papers? What do we think about the feminists in the limelight today? What do we

1

know that they don't know? And most important, what about us?

Are we proud of what we have achieved, or do we feel like failures? If we've made mistakes, is it because we were weak or foolish or confused, or is it because we didn't get the support we needed? Have we failed feminism or – to echo the classic backlash slogan – has feminism failed us?

How well have our interests been represented in feminist writing over the past two decades, and how well do feminist activists represent our interests in the world at large? Where do *we* think feminism should go from here, and how does that diverge from that suggested by our self-appointed leaders?

I am going to answer these general questions the only honest way I know – which is personally. I've decided to do this because one of the things that has always driven me crazy about feminist writing is its love affair with the floating generalisation. Most men do but shouldn't. Many women want but don't. Sometimes you have no choice but to say such things. You can't break ground for which no hard data exist without depending heavily on sweeping statements. Neither Mary Wollstonecraft nor Simone de Beauvoir could have left home without them. The problem is that their successors have shown little inclination to give them up. The books that result might be accurate expressions of our collective unconscious, but they rarely give a sense of what it's like to be alive here and now, or what happens to feminist ideals when you put them into practice. What happens to your life if you try, at least some of the time, to see the political in the personal.

This is what I'll be trying to describe in the pages that follow. This is my report from the trenches. Here is what I make of what I've done and what I've read and what I've witnessed and what I've discussed with my friends during sixteen years of bringing up children. It would have been nice, I suppose, if I could have gone out and interviewed a million working mothers representing all classes, ages, nationalities and ethnic groups. If I could now say to you this is not just what I believe, it is what all working mothers believe, regardless of their aspirations, circumstances, or lifestyle choices. But I put it to you that, even if I had taken that tack, it would still have been me, hiding behind them, and using them as mouthpieces. So instead I'll just say my piece and then you can decide whether or not you agree with me.

This is not an autobiography, although in places it reads like one. I draw from my experiences only where they pertain to the subject. This sounds dignified in theory. In fact it reads like dirty laundry – which is all very amusing unless it happens to be yours. One of the worst things about dirty laundry is that it rarely belongs just to you. If I could have written about my experiences as a mother without mentioning either my children or their fathers, or my friends, or their husbands and children, I certainly would have done so. The rule I've followed is to invade their privacy only when I can't make my point without doing so, and, given the choice, to invade mine first.

If my son's reaction is anything to go by, I have spoken against myself only too convincingly. One of the most embarrassing things I did in the course of researching the book was to exhume the diary I kept the first time I was pregnant. One of the most foolish things I did as a result was to read Matthew (the child who resulted) a few choice passages. He was appalled. 'Were you really that bad?' he asked. When I said yes, his next question was why had his father ever put up with me.

I tried to explain. 'I wasn't *that* bad,' I said. 'At least I was *trying* to get it right, and so was he. But you see, we were so idealistic. We were both sort of sleepwalking.'

Matthew's response to this was, 'God, that's terrible. When did you wake up?'

It was too long a story, I told him. But since that story ends where this one begins, I'll give you the short version, which goes like this:

I got married to Paul when I was twenty-three years old. Although we are both American, we were living in London.

Although he was only twenty-seven, Paul had already been married and divorced and published a book of short stories and an autobiography. Now he was working on a novel and so was I, between the numerous secretarial jobs from which I was always being fired, usually for refusing to be a quietly respectful female eunuch.

We had our first child when I was twenty-six. When Matthew was seven weeks old, we moved back to the US – first to Texas, then to California, Connecticut, and finally back to Texas. I published my first novel when Matthew was one and I was twenty-seven. I finished my second novel days before we had our second child, Emma.

By now I was thirty. When I was thirty-one, we moved back to England. When I was thirty-five, Paul and I got divorced – but both stayed in England. He moved to London, I stayed in Oxford. I had the children on weekdays. He had them at weekends. While I struggled with my third novel, I paid the bills by doing journalism. At first this was just book reviews. Then, by a fluke, I got a column. This meant spending time in the office.

Up until now I had worked mostly from home, my only outside contacts being in the genteel world of books. The friends I had who were not women were married to friends who were. Although we did not live in a state of perfect consensus, one thing we all agreed upon was that we all existed. But now, in the *real* real world of newspapers, I discovered that this simple fact was not commonly accepted.

My brief was to write about everyday life in some way that connected to trends and issues that had come up in the paper that week. But the trends and issues I chose to write about – simply because they were the ones that had come up at the school gate or outside some child or other's dance class – were not the ones my elders and betters seemed to be expecting. What *were* they expecting? All became clear when I wrote an article on what people I knew were saying about the Gulf War. Ian Jack, the editor I most admired, asked me, in the friendliest way, if I had made it all up. I told him that of course I hadn't. Why did he think that? Because, he said, mothers didn't discuss politics.

Oh we didn't, did we? He had to be joking. But it quickly became apparent that his colleagues were not. Mothers were interested in shopping, they told me, and clothes and child psychology and affairs of the heart. If they did ever pick up a paper, they jumped straight to the features. So I had to make up my mind. If I wanted to write about more serious matters, I had to get used to the fact that I was addressing a different audience. A different audience did not want to hear about mothers.

I did not get used to these facts. Instead, I decided to educate my bosses. They did not take well to the regime. They threatened to take the column away unless I got off the subject of mothers who discussed politics. I only pretended to see the wisdom of their instructions. I always made sure to include in every obedient column at least one secret joke at their expense. The one that pleased me the most was in a piece on self-help books. I wrote that I had noticed how friends used self-help titles – like, for example, *101 Ways to Find Out if Your Husband is Cheating on You* – to send messages to their loved ones. Then I sent a message to my employers by inventing the self-help title I claimed to have seen (female) friends brandishing lately in California when their (male) bosses stepped on them. It was called *Big Ego, Small Phallus*.

I got away with that one, but because I continued to write rebelliously, I lost the column two weeks after I gave birth to my third child, Helen. They told me over the phone it was all for the best. Hormones had made my already dangerously soft prose softer. I needed and deserved a rest. I would be happier, and enjoy my new baby more, without the pressure of a column. Yes, I shouted at the wall when I slammed down the receiver, but without the pressure of a column, how is the baby going to eat? They wanted me to go away quietly, I told my clenched fist; they wanted me to sink back into the ghetto where mothers never discuss politics. But there was never any chance of that happening, as I couldn't afford it.

Instead I learned how to write while breast-feeding. I finished a third and long-suffering novel, kept up the journalism, and did also manage to keep a roof over our heads. It wasn't even that hard – and that, I think, is why the feedback I got was so puzzling. Anything more than abject failure on my part seemed miraculous to people. All I had to do was make breakfast, and they said what a dynamo you are! Also puzzling was seeing the world again from behind a pushchair. Faced with a kerb that was too high or a doorway that was too narrow when I was wheeling around my first two children, I had said to myself: The real world has no room for me, I'll never belong to the real world again. But this time I just thought: What planet do these architects and urban planners live on?

By the time I had Helen I was thirty-eight. I was not living with Frank, Helen's father, at the time, but it was because of her that we moved in together soon afterwards. Frank is also American, but has been living in England since 1973. He is a university lecturer and teaches sociology. His two older children, Kimber and Rachel, are roughly the same age as my two older children. When we first moved in together, we chose a village halfway between Oxford, where mine were still at school, and Bath, where Frank taught and his children and their mother still lived. But the distances (1,000 miles of driving a week, all told) were crippling, so after eight months of commuter hell I decided, for the hundredth time since my first ill-fated attempt to combine home and work, that I had got it all wrong.

To put it all right, to turn us into a real family, I agreed to give up Oxford and move to Bath. We didn't have quite enough money to stretch to the rent we had to pay for the house in Bath that had enough studies and bedrooms for our huge new family, but I was convinced that, if I used my ingenuity, if I increased my productivity, and finished a book on fertility choices *and* an erotic novella in less than one year, if I found more reliable childcare, if I worked a forty- or fifty-hour week, and stayed cheerful, and got enough sleep, and ate right, and exercised, and really, *really* committed myself to the search for creative solutions, everything would work out all right for us. And not just all right for us, all right for women, men and children everywhere. All right for the future. I thought this because I still believed I was part of an important historical movement. I still thought my every movement counted. Even with my penchant for heavenly visions of solidarity, I could not have believed, not literally, that there was a pantheon of feminist foremothers watching over me and the rest of us, and proudly cheering us on, but I still thought that, metaphorically speaking, at least, we were all on the same side.

Then I got pregnant again and that was when I woke up.

Part One

My Case Against Feminism

1

THE PROBLEM WITH TOO MANY NAMES

The personal, *then* the political

This is how it happened: I was sitting at my kitchen table, trying to decide what to do about this unplanned, untimely, but not entirely accidental pregnancy, feeling pulled in a hundred directions by a thousand bullying emotions, and all the while pretending to read a newspaper, when I happened on an educational supplement on the abortion debate. It was attractively designed, with brightly coloured charts and carefully balanced bullet points. One page featured a drawing of a foetus. The opposite page featured a frowning woman who was clearly having difficulty thinking for herself, but persevering anyway. The concise explanatory essay resting at her feet quoted a pro-choice campaigner as saying that abortion was the cornerstone of feminism, because 'a woman has the right to plan her life the same way a man does'.

Now, I have been reading this statement, or statements like it, for going on twenty-five years. I've nodded absently, and moved on without missing a beat, in the way that you do when you come across a truth you hold to be self-evident. But on the occasion I'm describing, it struck me as a very odd way of putting it. I couldn't understand how the misery I was going through could be the cornerstone for anything.

Before I go any further, let me say what I do believe: that I could not even pretend to have control over my life if I did not have the right to abortion. Anyone who tries to take that right away from me or any woman is my enemy. So is anyone who tells me that I was put on earth for the sole purpose of raising children.

At the same time, I don't see why abortion has come to be celebrated as our single most important right. Forgive me if I've missed the point, but I thought feminism was about demanding equal opportunities, these to be backed up not just by the right to remain childless, but also by the right to have them if we so wish. If abortion is the cornerstone of feminism, the implication is that it is also a prerequisite. The suggestion is that we can only enjoy first-class citizenship to the extent that we agree to go without children. I can't see the wisdom in this. I understand, in a practical sense, why a man today can expect to have children without necessarily giving up anything, while for women it's a different story. But why does this unfair division of labour and privilege have to be confirmed inside feminist theory?

I asked around and was told that it wasn't. Feminism rose from the ashes in the late sixties, I was reminded, to challenge that very division. To prove that a woman did not have to choose between her biological destiny and her mind, or between work and motherhood. Didn't I remember all that talk about crèches? All that discussion about how important it was for both mothers and fathers to be equally involved in childrearing? Yes, I said, of course I remembered. When I marched into parenthood, it was with those very thought-balloons dangling over my head. These were even, despite my many failures, ideas I still believed in, that most of my friends still believed in. I would even go so far as to say we were obsessed with them. We have none of us figured out how to make motherhood into something other than ready-made oppression, but we don't see what feminism has to offer most women of the world unless we keep trying.

Over the past fifteen years, just about every conversation I have had with other mothers my age has led, in one way or another, to the same questions: How to do right by your children, your job, your partner, without undoing yourself. How to make them do right by you. How to balance things. When to put others first, when to be selfish. What's fair. What's not. What works, what's doomed. Who's responsible when and why and whose job it is to pay for it. It doesn't matter if the woman I am speaking to calls herself a feminist or not. The same applies to fathers, even those whose 'significant others' think they don't do enough, even those who are statistically categorised as 'absent'. We are all worried about the same things. But we worry inside ghettos. We seldom find our concerns reflected with any intelligence in the feminist debate.

When I was at university, the women's movement was dominated by women fifteen years older than I who were desperate to escape from motherhood. Now it is dominated by women fifteen years younger than I who hardly seem to realise that it exists. The problems we are discussing these days are the problems faced by eighteen year olds: how to date, what to do if an employer looks at you the wrong way. What rape is and isn't. Feminism is getting younger. And in regressing, it seems to have skipped over my generation without so much as a glance. Even when the great thinkers circle back to the perennial panfeminist abortion issue, it is framed in such a way as to make it almost unrecognisable to those of us who have moved beyond the world of adolescent eithers and ors.

It's a strange experience to stand on the sidelines of the abortion debate if you are in the process of considering the real thing. Even morning sickness becomes political and so twice as hard to bear. Both the pro-life and pro-choice arguments fuel fear. Most obviously, there is the politically dangerous fear of stopping what might become a life. Less obviously, there is the fear of babies, or, as many polite feminists insist on calling it, Biological Destiny. Listen to a pro-choice campaigner speak about the fate awaiting the victims of Biological Destiny and you'd think it was the name of a poison, or a dangerous hallucinogen that gives you an eighteen-year trip.

Listen also to what they say, in the abstract plural, of course, about the dangers posed by children. They wreck lives, curtail educations, rob their mothers of adolescence, jobs, and travel opportunities. They eat bank accounts for breakfast. These arguments might be plausible to an adolescent – certainly they had me convinced when I was an adolescent – but if you've had children before, you know there's more to it than that, even in the event of your worst-case scenario coming true.

Nobody wants to have an abortion. It is, as any good family-planning agency will tell you, an insurance policy that exists to underwrite the other less extreme reproductive choices.

To cover accidents and mistakes. But there are accidents and accidents, mistakes and mistakes. Sometimes you know what you're doing, and sometimes you don't. Sometimes you don't want to know. Sometimes you rewrite history. Sometimes you know for sure that your life has no room for a baby. And sometimes . . .

. . . Sometimes you just develop an irrational hatred of your diaphragm. Sometimes, instead of inserting it, you send it flying across the bathroom floor. This is what I had done. Why? Who knows? Maybe because I secretly wanted a baby. Maybe because twenty years of contraceptive compliance is more than any normal woman can take. Maybe the thing I feared most is not having a baby but planning one. If you end up getting pregnant from mixed feelings, what is the right and responsible course? This was what I was trying to figure out that morning at my kitchen table.

As I agonised about whether or not I deserved this baby, whether or not this baby deserved me, whether I had the right to inflict it on the unconsulted father, and whether or not I would be risking the welfare of the existing children by continuing such a recklessly conceived pregnancy – as I asked myself how I could even consider depriving this innocent, unsuspecting collection of cells of the chance of life simply because my feet were feeling cold – as I meandered from confusion into bathos, my reason was further weakened by what I can only call feminist paranoia. I was my own worst enemy. No matter what I did, I now ran an equal risk of ruining my life. Whatever went wrong as a result of this compulsive gamble, I would only have myself to blame. But even this exercise in self-flagellation was complicated by the equally strong conviction that I had become the victim of my own idealistic diligence. If I had stayed at home and put my feet up and let the men worry about the money, I would have had the time and the space to have this child, and probably even its father's approval. But because I had gone out there and acted on this idea that economic autonomy would allow me to plan my own life just like a man did, I now found myself, paradoxically, without the time or money to justify another child. If I did not avail myself of the cornerstone of feminism, in other words, I was going to find myself outside its jurisdiction.

To make a long and droning story short, I decided to have the baby anyway. You could say it was my way of saying fuck you, I'll do it my way. I would say that what decided me in the end was a tug so immune to reason, so very different from the love I've felt for real babies, that I blushed for fear of being found out every time a doctor said, 'It's your decision. What do you want?'

I got to hear that a lot over the months and genetic tests that followed. My personal sampling of the reproductive choices that were open to me went on further to tarnish my feelings about that upper-case goal, Reproductive Choice. This is a concept that glitters only when in the plural and hypothetical. Face a real choice and there are risks, losses, sacrifices. Unforeseen consequences. Surprise emotions, regrets, and numbers that place you beyond the reach of reason. Now you're looking at odds of 200 to 1 that your child might exhibit Deformity A. Now suddenly, it's another dread outcome, and odds of 841 to 23. It is when I was obliged to handicap my future as if it were a temperamental horse that I began to see how large the gap was between the realities of Reproductive Choice and the ideal. And asked myself whose big idea it was to offer Reproductive Choice as the talisman we must wear to fend off Biological Destiny.

What the hell *is* Biological Destiny, anyway? It sounds medieval. But here it is parading around inside the main feminist argument for the right to abortion.

It's not the only term in this debate that demands a closer look. When choices combine and ossify to become Choice, the words we use to describe the consequences of real choices become abstractions, too. And when losses, regrets and sacrifices move into the abstract, then it starts to sound as if Loss, Regret, and Sacrifice are not so much consequences of a particular action, but the price of admission to the world in which women 'can plan their lives just as men do'.

When the right to choose becomes Choice, there follows also a general lack of interest in the consequences of individual choices exercised. A sense of ideological stalling. A refusal to budge, as it were, from the display window. A failure, therefore, to tackle the real injustices that are built into just about every reproductive choice on offer.

I call this syndrome 'menu feminism'. I take my inspiration from Joan Didion. I'm sure you remember that essay she wrote in *The White Album*, in which she said feminism was not a movement but a symptom. In another passage from the same offending essay, she likened the lack of a political game-plan in feminism to a similar problem she had noticed in civil rights. She said that there were times when she wondered if all its leaders ever aspired to was the right to sit side by side with their oppressors at the same lunch counter.[1]

An unkind remark, I hear you say. I agree, and I join with you, I'm sure, in hoping that it's also untrue. Certainly access is an important first step for any group that has hitherto been excluded from the centres of power, but for many great feminist thinkers, it also appears to have been the last. As far as I can see, most of them are still at that lunch counter, obsessing over the choices on the board, and living in mortal fear that the management may try, when their backs are turned, to erase today's special offer. Frozen inside this vision of the struggle, they fail to notice that each and every item is fashioned from half a loaf – and costs a woman twice what it will cost a man.

When these self-appointed soul sisters rap on about fending off Biological Destiny, what they are really trying to fend off is the day when they will have to face the news that freedom and justice are more than a hysterectomy away.

Our feminist canon tells us that an unplanned, unintended, unwanted or ill-timed baby is likely to 'ruin' a mother's life. Any woman who has gone on to give birth to one of the above in spite of these dire warnings can tell you that, actually, it's not the baby who ruins your life, but everyone else. It's the family who won't stand by you. It's the headmistress who expels you. The employer who sacks you during maternity leave, the unplanned father who fails to rise to this occasion in the same way that he rose to the invitation that started it. It's the midwife, the doctor, the health visitor who assumes, until other evidence emerges, that you are a social problem. It's the politician who rants on about immorality while refusing to extend the protection of employment law. It's the school system that bases its schedules on the assumption that every child has a full-time mother. The bigot who thinks babies should be breast-fed in public toilets.

The shoe manufacturer who bankrupts you by forecasting the pitter-patter of crippled feet. The door that refuses to admit a double pushchair. The car-park that's built on an incline. The city planner who has a thing about steps.

It is not that these narrows doors, sloping concrete vistas, and killer stairways exist expressly to impede us. There is not a mad architect out there thinking: Now, if I design this car-park on an incline, or put steps right here, I can really make a headache for working single mothers who have the gall to put their groceries into trolleys. No, there are hundreds and thousands of nice architects of both genders, who just don't want to know. They don't want to know, because if they did know they'd have to change the way they designed things.

The feminist canon has it that we are the great beneficiaries if we can escape Biological Destiny. When, actually, everyone else benefits even more. They get to continue business as usual. Run things just the way they did in the good old days when mothers and their children stayed quietly at home.

When we set out to tame ourselves biologically, we're accepting the very destiny we set out to challenge. We are using what I call Chamberlain Logic, because what it amounts to is appeasement.

Let's face it. If the world were arranged to support parents' needs, there would be no problem combining work with the rearing of children. If we owned a share of the restaurant, we'd be writing the menu. If we owned the building, we would not be straining to learn the right language to speak to the management. We would be ordering what we need and just getting on with it. We have our friends as well as our enemies to thank for the fact that all of the above are hopeless fantasies. By reducing procreation to the status of a costly optional extra, the women's movement has left mothers in the lurch.

Sure, we get the usual Mother's Day-type tributes – but frankly, they are even less convincing than the ones we used to get from fifties patriarchs. We rise above the pity line every once in a while, as victims of domestic violence, sexual harassment, or unusually low wages. But there is little interest in the more complex problems presented by the double load, still less interest in any insights we have to offer. If our situation fails to illustrate some aspect of the war between the sexes, it fails to capture the feminist imagination. When we say yes, but what about childcare, what about campaigning to get all working mothers protected by employment law, we get the brush-off. From the sighs and rolling eyeballs, you would think we were back in the fifties suburb that women invented feminism to escape from. We are made to feel like nagging children who have interrupted a fascinating discourse on Ring Around the Collar with an unnecessary request for juice.

Why is this? It's because the femstars with their hands on the microphones are almost all childless, or to use their latest buzzword, child-free. With very few exceptions, the household-name feminists with children are the ones who fell into the rut before the movement began, and for whom motherhood was therefore a given, and a condition to outgrow. These child-free and post-rut feminists are not interested in the problems of contemporary childrearing because these questions do not touch their own lives. Fair enough, you might say. But it seems to me that they have turned their small personal prejudices into a large and dangerous political blind spot.

How did it come to this?

The simple ahistorical answer is that their small personal prejudices sell books. The simple historical answer is that the mother of the modern feminist blockbuster, Betty Friedan, learned all her tricks from the demon advertisers whose 'sexual sell' she sought to expose in *The Feminine Mystique*. The formula she used in this book is a variation on the formula her less idealistic mentors used to create markets for deodorant and mouthwash. My name for it is 'Disease and Cure'. There's something rotten in Denmark, Britain, suburbia, our treacherous hearts. To quote Betty: a problem with no name. Having lowered our defences and aroused our morbid curiosity, she whams us with a diagnosis. We are weak, childish, unfulfilled, inauthentic. Our courage has failed us. We are not fully human. Every breath we take is a lie. We don't even know what love is. We can't even mother properly. And if we don't take action now, we'll

MY CASE AGAINST FEMINISM

pass the disease on to our children. But don't worry, she says (once she has us grovelling in a panic of self-loathing), there is a way forward. It's not our fault. It's just the way we were brought up. We must subject ourselves to a remake. Change our attitude. Promise not to be so passive, so dependent, so woefully incomplete. And buy this terrific new package, the Betty Friedan life-plan.

Which makes sublime sense, if you happen to be a member of her original target audience – in other words, a fifties suburbanite with three children and a never-dusted college degree. But if you're twenty years younger, or come from another country, or don't have quite so much money as she does, then it's immediately clear that she's not just selling feminism. She is also selling her oppressive cultural blinkers. If we're going to follow her instructions, we're also going to have to become good little middle-class WASPs.

You could argue that it is unkind to take her book out of its context. That we must appreciate it for what it accomplished. If Betty hadn't used her skills to commercialise feminism, the ideas would never have spread in the way that they have. They would have remained locked up inside the ivory tower where Virginia Woolf sits Rapunzel-like in a room she calls her own. Today, thanks to Betty, they have found their way into kitchens across the world. I accept the importance of taking feminism to the masses, but I would like to remind you that just about every feminist blockbuster writer you can think of is, in fact, a graduate of an ivory tower. If they don't have Ivy League degrees, they have Oxbridge degrees. Quite a few have both. When they talk to the general public, they talk down to it in the same way that their male peers do. They are, in other words, not just middle class in their assumptions, but also elitist.

It ought to come as no surprise, then, that the audience for these books comes out of the same schools. Since the late sixties, the ideal reader for a feminist blockbuster is a university student whose beliefs are in disarray after a few months without parental guidance, and who is desperate for a more exciting, more accepting guide to explain the world to her. The guide I found when I answered to that description was Germaine Greer. She was the one who told me it was all right to be sexual, and to experiment, and to take myself seriously even when I was having fun. She was the one who taught me how to hold my own in any company, and so I suppose I should be grateful to her. But when I go back to *The Female Eunuch* now I am appalled by her bossiness. By the aggressiveness with which she sells the Germaine-brand Utopian package. And if you don't believe me, dig out your copy, and turn to the last chapter, when Big Sister tells us how to get liberated.

Out of the house! she barks, as briskly as a games mistress. 'Most women still need a room of their own and the only way to find it may be outside their own homes.'[2] Having marshalled her troops, she tells us in one breath that we are free to follow our own inclinations, and then in the next breath that, oh, by the way, it will all come to nothing unless we promise to (a) reject our role as principal consumers in the capitalist state, (b) refuse to accept the masculine/feminine polarity, (c) boycott hairdressers, (d) throw away our false eyelashes, (e) get real about make-up. From now on, it must be 'strictly for fun'. Expensive French concoctions are out, it therefore follows. We are to limit ourselves to kohl, spirit of camphor, oil of cloves and frankincense, crumbled lavender, patchouli and attar of roses.[3] And when we dress to kill, we must keep our wits about us and *go* for that kill. *Especially* in the company of men, and *especially* at the pub, we must make full use of our sharp tongues.

But not against just anybody. Oh, perish the thought! When Big Sisters talk, we ignore them at our peril:

> Experience is too costly a teacher: we cannot all marry in order to investigate the situation. The older sisters must teach us what they found out. At all times we must learn from each other's experience . . . We must fight against the tendency to form a feminist elite, or a masculine-type authority in our own political structures, and struggle to maintain co-operation and the matriarchal principle of fraternity.[4]

Must, must, must. It's not good enough just to go through the motions. You have to have the right attitude. Thought can be a crime. To quote Big Sister once again: 'The surest guide to the correctness of the path that women take is joy in the struggle. Revolution is the festival of the oppressed.'[5]

This is the type of advice that makes me want to go home and iron boxer shorts. Honestly, Germaine. You make revolution sound about as much fun as a square-dancing lesson. And when you talk about the dangers lurking on the other side of our (your) chosen path – you remind me of that elderly virgin who used to chaperone our school parties, who used to stalk the dance floor with a flashlight doing spot checks on hands she suspecting of wandering.

Don't listen to what men say, she warns us. Don't listen to women either, unless that woman is Germaine:

Privileged women will pluck at your sleeve and seek to enlist you in the 'fight' for reforms, but reforms are retrogressive. Bitter women will call you to rebellion, but you have too much to do.

Which is when she throws down her parting challenge, the question that may have ruined my life: 'What *will* you do?'[6] It occurs to me now that the real question at this juncture was not *what* we would do, but (having left home with only our purest cosmetics and said bridge-burning goodbyes to all our oppressors) where we expected to be doing it, and how we were going to pay for it. Alas, it is not a question our Bettys and our Germaines ever really address, for the simple reason that they have never known poverty. Since becoming media figurines, they hardly even know what it's like to be middle class.

What they do know, and know well, is how to work the media. They, and their disciples, know the importance of a hook and a courtroom drama. To sell sexual harassment, you need Anita Hill. To sell the idea of female retribution, you need to find a penis on a lonely intersection. And maybe they're right. Maybe we do need to milk every sex scandal for everything it's worth. These are the stories that make feminism interesting. Alas, they are also the stories that make my problems look/ boring.

The changes that would make my life better are really quite straightforward. Good childcare. Protection under employment law. Better pay. Despite the fact that I have a florid imagination, I have yet to find a way to make my case look like a sex vendetta. No, even when I am at my most fervent, I speak of these things, and people see missionary spectacles. Tweed skirts. Support stockings. Sturdy brown shoes. In trying so hard to make itself punchy and provocative, blockbuster feminism perpetuates the myths that hold us back.

One of these myths is the eternal patriarchal conspiracy. It was invented by Kate Millett, revived by Marilyn French and Andrea Dworkin, and made respectable by Catharine MacKinnon. The problem with no name here is a war that has been waging for millennia, invisibly but, paradoxically, under our noses. No need to say on whom this war is being waged or by whom. And no need to insist on footnotes or bibliographies – who wants to get lost in arid and reflexive conventions of patriarchal scholarship when you know instinctively that your hunches are right? No need either to confine yourselves to the modern context. They dignify their grand designs by goosestepping back into prehistory, a Never-neverland of even greater certainties. Men were marginal in those days. The abuse of women only began after horticulture. How to correct millennia of injustice? Oh, that's as easy as twisting a fact. Think of the historical record as one big bring-and-buy sale. Find a nice buzzword, second-hand but good as new, and recite it. Resistance. Resistance. Resistance. If anyone gets up the nerve to ask what it means in practical terms, just wave your hand vaguely and say in a disdainful voice that it depends on the context. If anyone should dare to say actually, I suspect life may be more complicated than you suggest, just follow the Kate Millett precedent, and here I'm quoting from the first page of *Sexual Politics*:

> Much here, and throughout the book, is tentative, and in its zeal to present a consistent argument has omitted (although it need not preclude) the more familiar ambiguities and contradictions of our social arrangements.[7]

I don't know about everybody else, but I personally would have appreciated more discussion about how to negotiate these vexing ambiguities and contradictions. I mean, you can't go around telling people to change their lives because the personal is political, and then throw up your hands and say sorry, sisters! These complications have given me the biggest headache! Forgive me, but that's an even bigger cop-out than motherhood.

I'll take the war book any day, though, over the 'I spy all the problems of the world in my own little ego' book. I'm talking here about books like *The Cinderella Complex*, *Women Who Love Too Much*, and yes, how could I forget it, *Revolution from Within*. Their formula is even more insidious than Kate Millett-type male scapegoating, because it implies that we don't have equality because we are poor spiritual housekeepers. It goes like this: 'Oh, hi, I'm a discontented product of my environment. I got to the age of thirty, and found out I had made such a big mistake about love/men/work/children/ nurturing/feminism/ambition. So I went and interviewed a lot of friends and friends of friends and rigged the questions so that they would parrot my own answers. That convinced me we had all made the same mistake! In my quest to find out why, I went back to the same genius who was so very wrong about penis envy, and found out it was all in the early childhood department of our heads! But because I am a forward-looking person, I threw in a few recommendations about changes that must occur in the structuring of family, workplace and government.'

The personal is not just political, in other words – it's also a cartoon. That's not the whole story – of course not! Men must change too, they say portentously. (Notice the refusal to move out of the plural.) And so must institutions, also plural and unspecified. We have no idea how we're going to make these vaguely defined oppressors bow to our will. But we hope eventually they'll identify themselves and come round. But in the meantime, we can optimise our own personal chances with a better self-image, and a new lifeplan.

Sounds like a twenty-one-day diet, doesn't it? You could say that that is all you're bound to get so long as feminist blockbusters follow advertising guidelines. You could also say that we got what we needed from them – a desire for equality, an understanding of the political nature of our exploitation, a set of guidelines for experimentation, even this idea that mothers could and were well advised to work. You could say that this legacy is all that matters. I put it to you that we have also inherited some pretty gruesome ideas about woman's traditional lot.

Our great foremothers on the subject of motherhood

Let's begin with Mary Wollstonecraft. To say she had a low opinion of her female contemporaries is an understatement. They were so ignorant, so slavishly ruled by pleasure, and so desperate for male admiration that they were not just bad mothers, but dangerous ones, too:

> The want of natural affection in many women, who are drawn from their duty by the admiration of men, and the ignorance of others, renders the infancy of man a much more perilous state than that of brutes.[8]

It is only fair to point out that the duty her middle-class peers were avoiding was breast-feeding, that their reason for doing so was to spend more time with men, and that the danger their children ran while in the care of wet nurses was a higher chance of death. Although she had a hard time controlling her distaste and her disapproval for their wanton ways, she did not hold them personally responsible. Women were systematically weakened by men, she said, and then corrupted. One tragedy led to another:

> The weak enervated women who particularly catch the attention of libertines are unfit to be mothers, though they may conceive, so that the rich sensualist, who has rioted among women, spreading depravity and misery, when he wishes to perpetuate his name, receives from his wife only an half-formed being, that inherits both its father's and mother's weakness.[9]

Despite her rather worrying worries on breeding and good genetic stock, and her just as worrying equating of pleasure and ignorance, she did sincerely want to improve the lot of mothers. She was convinced that a good education would better equip them to overcome their traditional failings. Alas, a century and a half later, a chorus of ungrateful daughters emerged to say that the experiment hadn't worked. 'Maternity,' Simone de Beauvoir informed us in *The Second Sex*, 'is usually a strange mixture of narcissism, altruism, idle daydreaming, sincerity, bad faith, devotion and cynicism.'[10] It was a condition to be avoided by any woman who sought to become 'authentic'. She could understand a woman who became pregnant by accident, but for the multiparous like me her contempt brought out the poet in her: we are 'fowls with high production,' she snorts, 'who seek eagerly to sacrifice their liberty of action for the functioning of their flesh.'[11]

You would have thought Betty Friedan would be a little softer on the idea, seeing as she herself had children by the time she sat down to write *The Feminine Mystique*. But no. Educated women who bought the fifties package and stayed at home to devote themselves entirely to their husbands and children were suffering from a 'massive sickness of sex without self'.[12] Using her favourite rhetorical device, the open question for which there is only one admissible answer, she asks:

> Just as college girls used the sexual fantasy of married life to protect them from the conflicts and growing pains and work of a personal commitment to science, or art, or society, are these married women putting into their insatiable sexual search the aggressive energies which the feminine mystique forbids them to use for larger human purposes? Are they using sex or sexual fantasy to fill needs that are not sexual?[13]

She goes on to bemoan, *à la* Wollstonecraft, the example they are setting: 'The tragedy of children acting out the sexual fantasies of their housewife mothers is only one sign of the progressive dehumanisation that is taking place.'[14]

Germaine Greer is even less forgiving of maternal error than Betty: 'When children are falsely presented to women as the only significant contribution, the proper expression of their creativity, and their lives' work, the children and their mothers suffer for it,' she says.[15] Again, the children suffer most:

> Energy does seem diabolical to us, because our whole culture is bent on harnessing it for ulterior ends: the child must be civilized; what this means is really he must be obliterated. From the beginning he is discouraged from crowing and exercising his lungs at any time or in any place where it might inconvenience adult discourse. The new baby has enormous curiosity and an equal faculty for absorbing information, but he spends all of it on specially constructed environments featuring muted sounds, insipid colours and the massive dominating figure of Mother.[16]

It is not just the child's tragedy that he is forced to be both 'her toy and her achievement'. Our society is sick, Germaine bawls, because it:

> ... insists upon Mother's domination as a prerequisite for character formation. The child's attention must be weaned away from exterior reality on to an introverted relationship of mutual exploitation which will form the pattern of his future compulsions.[17]

Although *he* will fare much better than *she* will:

> While little boys are learning about groups and organisations as well as the nature of the world outside their homes, little girls are at home, keeping quiet, playing with dolls and dreaming, or helping Mother. At school they use their energy to suppress themselves, to be good and keep quiet, and remember what they are hearing and doing. At home they perform meaningless physical rituals, with no mental activity attached to them. So the sensual and intellectual are even more widely separated in them than they are in their brothers. If the sensual retains its hold, they prefer to work with their hands, cooking, sewing, knitting, following a pattern designed by someone else. The designers, the master

cooks, and the tailors are men. If women become intellectuals they are disenfranchised of their bodies, repressed, intense, inefficient, still as servile as ever . . .[18]

Although, on the evidence here, the future would be a safer place if they chose this cul-de-sac rather than perpetuating their horrible legacy by becoming Mothers themselves. How to reproduce the human race without perpetuating the evils of maternity? This was a problem G.G. confessed to being awfully bothered about. She was particularly worried about the fact that brilliant women were not passing on their genes:

In a situation where a woman might contribute a child to a household which engages her attention for part of the time while leaving her free to frequent other spheres of influence, brilliant women might be more inclined to reproduce.[19]

Her own dream solution, she confessed, would be a beautiful counterculture farmhouse in the Italian countryside. The house and land could be worked by a local family. She and friends with 'similar problems' could stay there when 'circumstances permitted' and when they were to give birth. 'Perhaps some of us might live there for long periods, as long as we wanted to.' The children's 'fathers and other people would also visit the house as often as they could, to rest and enjoy the children and even work a bit'. The children, meanwhile, would be free to roam and form valuable relationships with many adults, while – in sharp contrast to children on Kibbutzim – also exploring their sexuality with their peers if and when they so wished. Just as they would not own their parents, their parents would not own them, and so not pass on to them their wretched neuroses:

If necessary the child need not even know that I was his womb-mother and I could have relationships with the other children as well. If my child expressed a wish to try London or New York or go to formal school somewhere, that could also be tried without committal . . .[20]

What a nightmare.

It's important to remember, though, that you could not call yourself a feminist in those days unless you were prepared to drone on and on about brave new families

un true

It was almost a signature tune. In the sixties and seventies, the family was the one thing that radical, liberal, Marxist, and psychoanalytic feminists agreed about. It had to be changed, drastically and at once, or else the sky was going to fall. The arguments were about how to perform the emergency rescue. Make the personal political, said the early radicals, and you destroy the line that has kept women privately exploited throughout the ages. Keep men out, said their successors, and while you're at it, boycott any friends who resort to the evil tradition of marriage. Expose the feminine mystique, said the liberals, and you can free women to explore their full potential. Sit back, let the contradictions deepen, and wait for the apocalypse, said the Marxists. While the psychoanalytics said it's simply a matter of figuring how we've been mismanaging the Oedipal crisis.

Communes! cried the chorus. As the pioneers struggled to find new ways of living without the old evils of sexism, the Utopians went to work on a fine new range of communities for them to aspire to. These ranged from male-free heavens on the lesbian continuum, where sperm never ventured beyond the test tube, to Shulamith Firestone's limited-contract households that would merge at the right time into a joyous, polymorphously perverse society freed from the incest taboo, to the future suggested by French theorists like Elisabeth Badinter in which the sexes almost merge and social structures mirror their concern with sharing and caring, and lust, once again, is no longer a problem – and men can bear children.[21]

The golden rule for these feminist Utopians – and this has been so since Charlotte Perkins Gilman's *Herland* – was isolate the ingredient that makes the traditional family sick, and then make the cake again without the offending men, or the overbearing mothers, or the repressed children. Looking at the family to locate what it did well was just not on. Betty Friedan forgot this rule when she wrote *The Second Stage* – and she is still getting her knuckles rapped for it. Which brings me to the next chapter in my depressing survey of the feminist literature on motherhood.

A tale of two blockbusters

Betty Friedan never saw *The Second Stage* as a reversal of *The Feminine Mystique*. Rather, she thought of it as an effort to correct an imbalance it inadvertently helped to cause. The first stage of the Friedan plan, she reminded us in oracular tones, had been all about integrating the workplace. Now that we had achieved that task (!) and now that we had also developed our personhoods (!!) the time had come to reassess the treacherous hearth. Looking back, she had decided that some of our previously suspect 'soft' domestic values were worth preserving and could find good use outside as well as inside the home. We also had to decide who was going to look after the children. We needed to embark on both these projects with men:

> And this new *human* liberation will enable us to take back the day *and* the night, and use the precious, limited resources of our earth and the limitless resources of our human capital to erect new and old family bonds that can evolve and nourish us through all the changes of our lives, and use the time that is our life to enrich our human possibility, spelling our own names, at last, as women and men.[22]

She sent her Adams and her Eves off on their journey of togetherness with a number of serious questions unanswered. (1) How to make men (without whom a wholesale egalitarian Utopia cannot happen) even slightly interested in feminist-directed human liberation? (2) How to oblige the workplace, wherever that is, to adjust to an increasingly female, and increasingly casual, female workforce that will be far easier to exploit if it refuses to adjust? (3) How to figure out what mothers have been doing behind the veil of silence since time began so that we can give credit where credit is due, give the people who look after children today the time and space and support they need to do it, and keep things going when they're not there?

Anyone who lives in the real world knows that any strategy leaving these questions unanswered is doomed to *reductio ad absurdum* and therefore failure. But that's not what the uproar was about when the book came out. The uproar was how dare Betty back out on us and send us back in that rut? She had dared to speak hopefully about mothers, fathers, and families. She had dared to ask uncomfortable questions about who was going to look after the children. She got neither the audience nor the debate nor the trend she had hoped for.

But there was someone else around who did know how to play the game and did know how to disguise her radical suggestions in acceptable disguises. Carol Gilligan, the messiah of that eighties publishing phenomenon, Difference Feminism, brought out *In a Different Voice* at about the same time Betty Friedan brought out *The Second Stage*. Where Betty got disappointed reviews and curt dismissals, Carol created a very different kind of storm. The vicious attacks from equal-rights hardliners were nicely muffled by the huge, almost too grateful sighs of relief from everyone else. She was even *Ms Magazine*'s Woman of the Year. Her thesis, which was a psychological variation on Betty's liberal, populist sermon, was that girls answered to a different code of ethics. Girls cared more about maintaining connections when they were confronted with ethical dilemmas, while boys were more concerned with honouring abstract principles of justice. This did not make girls superior or inferior – only different. If psychological models found that girls didn't rate as well on their developmental scales, it was because the scales did not account for this difference. They expected girls to act like boys. The only way forward was to change the scales so that they reflected both modes of development. The standard of maturity could remain the same – a well-rounded adult was one who could integrate the traditionally male ethic of natural rights with the traditionally female ethic of care and community connections. Her point was that girls and boys tended to approach this goal from different starting points.

In a climate where difference was just another word for inequality, she was putting herself on the line just by using it. So she was wise and very very clever not to speak out in favour of the Ethic of Care while stranding herself in the domestic realm where most people learn it. Instead of looking at how mothers consciously acted on and interpreted this ethic, instead of trying to work out how they actively brought up both their daughters and their sons to respect humane values, instead of asking if their apparently greater success with their daughters had something to do with the very different instructions both daughters and sons got from people outside the home, she chose instead to base her claims on feminist gender-formation theory.

This is the theory, developed by Nancy Chodorow,[23] that women are worse at autonomy and better at relationships simply because most children are brought up by women and mother–daughter attachments are harder to break. According to the theory, gender formation is something that happens unconsciously. It is an Oedipal drama that cannot be overcome or skipped through exercise of the will. It assumes, therefore, that the Ethic of Care does not depend on thought, conviction, practice, trial or error.

If Carol Gilligan had done studies of active mothers, she would have had to challenge these assumptions or develop her theory further to explain them. Instead, Gilligan took the diplomatic way out and did studies with schoolgirls, young adults, and women deciding whether or not to have abortions – all people who were in situations that allowed them a certain detachment from their families, and whose deliberations did not directly challenge the idea that the Ethic of Care was set in granite during early childhood.

Gushes of books have resulted from the Carol Gilligan revolution. Many have drawn radical conclusions from it.[24] But even the most daring of the faithful have not challenged the Granite Gender Theory directly. The only ones who seem to entertain any doubts about it are the people who have retained the old left and even older equal rights suspicions about families. The new femstars have inherited these traditions.

*   *   *

What do the intrepid acrobats of the new wave have to say on the subject of motherhood?

Yes – what line are your Faludis taking on these difficult issues? And your Wolfs? Your Roiphes? Your Paglias and postmodernists?

They're outside playing 'Let's Just Pretend It Isn't Happening'. Let's Just Pretend that an entire generation of feminist mothers does not exist, or not in human form, anyway – having emerged from the labour ward with marshmallows for brains.

Where do people like us figure, for example, in *Backlash*? It's never clear if Susan Faludi thinks we are cracking the whip or bearing the brunt of it. The main reason behind her crusade is to show how women have been scared into premature motherhood with false stories about men shortages, infertility epidemics and birth dearths. How dare they? she howls. How dare Betty Friedan even backtrack on her seminal work to suggest that the domestic realm contained traditions worth preserving? Then, in the same breath, she howls, how dare anyone even suggest that equal-rights feminism undervalues mothers? She cites as an example its longstanding endorsement of daycare centres. What is this claptrap, she asks, about NOW not being interested in the needs of mothers? How can that be true, she asks, if, in the early seventies, it campaigned for *five* whole daycare packages in Congress?[25] If we fail to be impressed by this astonishing achievement, we open ourselves to a barrage of abuse that would, if it came from Norman Mailer, be enough to put him behind bars. There are times when she reads as if her main source of childcare issues *was* Norman Mailer. The idea that there might be more to childcare than daycare has simply not occurred to her. It has simply not occurred to her, I would guess, because she has never had sole responsibility for a young child.

She herself is not against mothers *per se*. But she just can't make up her mind about us either. We're heroines when challenged by advocates of foetal rights, and martyrs to be championed when we work for a chemical factory that requires us to get sterilised if we want to keep working with substances that might adversely affect our reproductive systems. But if any film or TV programme dares to present us as valuing homes, relationships or children, the dragon's nostrils flame with fury. Nesting shows! she hisses. Regressive fantasies! She approves of us only to the extent that we continue to work. In her postadolescent world, work is something that mothers do for feminist, not economic reasons. She also seems to assume that when her fellow Americans with children do work, they use daycare and not undocumented workers. This is because she only knows the official story. She doesn't know the unofficial story because she has not yet paid a visit to our ghetto on the dark side of the moon.

But at least our problems occasionally come up on her screen. On Naomi Wolf's screen we don't even register as blips. Which makes reading *The Beauty Myth* an almost surreal experience for any woman over thirty-five. Every time I pick it up I experience a profound sense of *déjà lu*. The stuff about women being desexed by patriarchal culture – surely it was Germainè Greer who said that? The stuff on the glorious social transformations that will follow from truly egalitarian heterosexual love – not even Germaine would have been *that* naive! The political connotations of rape – isn't that sanitised Brownmiller and Dworkin? This stuff about saying no to frivolous fashion, and yes to dress-for-success uniforms – wouldn't even Brownmiller agree that it's all rather grim – not to mention accommodating? I hear she calls her book a classic Marxist analysis. I call it ahistorical materialism.

How lucky I am, I think, to have been born when I was. And thus to have missed out on anorexia. Except that I didn't miss out on it. Although by her figures I predate the epidemics, I had swarms of anorexic and bulimic classmates. If the epidemics predated second-wave feminism, how can she say they were caused by the anti-feminist backlash? She can say that, I'm afraid, because as far as she's concerned, my generation doesn't exist.

Am I a slave to the beauty myth? I should be so lucky. Lack of funds has saved me from the liposuction and face-lift dilemmas. I suspect the same is true for most of my peers. Oh, but, dear me, I do regular exercise! Can it be that in doing so I am wasting time and money in the vain pursuit of lost youth? I always thought that I did this to keep healthy, because if I'm not healthy, who's going to keep the household going? I always thought exercise fell under the heading of doing something for myself. That it was an alternative to sitting at home and looking after children. Why doesn't it look this way to Naomi Wolf? Because she has never had to sit at home and look after children, yet.

America has experienced a gender quake, she announces in her new one, *Fire with Fire*. When Anita Hill accused Clarence Thomas of sexual harassment, the women of the nation stood up, and said we're not going to take it any more! They decided to get more women into political office. When Emily began to compile her List, one of the first to make a big donation was Naomi Wolf. In order to do so, she had to unlearn all sorts of bad attitudes about money and power. Once she had overcome her handicap, she helped set up a network so that she and her friends could help each other overcome these bad habits together, and pick up good habits, too! If women are going to get ahead, she says originally, they have to learn to be nice to each other.

She has some not very nice things to say, though, about the way girls traditionally treat each other in the playground – ruling by clique consensus, punishing anything less than total obedience with exclusion. They act this way, she says, inadvertently echoing the New Age-feminist-pop-Jungian Clarissa Pinkola Estes, because by the time they get to the age of eight, they have already learned how to suppress their wild side.

And perhaps this is true. I certainly have vivid and unhappy memories about the cliques of eight- and nine-year-old girls who would not speak to me if I was ever so bold as to wear the wrong colour socks. But this idea she has about women being unable to network – can she be serious? How the hell does she think those of us with children manage? Everything I know about children, everything I know about the places where I've lived, I know through the maternal networks I have belonged to. Mothers network to help each other, with backup in emergencies, with information about useful people and services, with emotional support as one childcare crisis follows another. The trust without which these networks could not exist comes based on an unspoken, ironclad consensus about what is safe and suitable for children and what is not. In other words, my long-ago playground education in female-group obedience may have had at least one good outcome. What do you think, Naomi?[26]

But Naomi does not think. No, as far as she is concerned, there is nothing to discuss. Feminist writers demystified motherhood decades ago. These days, men and women bring up children together. Her parents had no trouble doing this – it follows, therefore, that no one else has either. Yes, she's troubled about abortion, but only because it has so often implied, at least for her friends, a previous episode involving *less than perfect contraceptive vigilance*. I am a real spacey person, she says, but I've never slipped up in this department! She claims that this was because an abortion was not a decision she ever wished to face. She boasts that she has always been clear about her need to avoid pregnancy. In the course of her four-page discussion, she does not once mention the words 'baby' or 'mother'.[27]

So it is a relief to turn to Katie Roiphe, who gives such great importance to her mother, and to the changes that occur between one generation and another. Here, for once, you have a sense of the difficulty of legacy. The metaphysical choice facing her is not to have children/or to have a career, but which feminist tradition to claim as her own. She sees herself caught between the good mothers (feminists like her own mother who believed in experimentation and accountability) and the bad mothers (Catharine MacKinnon and the anti-porn crusaders). She worries about how she is going to make her life her own in time for the hazy day, ten years off, when all her friends file 'two by two into the Noah's Ark of adulthood'.[28] But you wonder how many of them will dare. Settling down and having children is what you do after the story is over.

In this story, she slumps oh so regretfully in the shadow of the feminist world she believes her mother to have inhabited. The greatest tragedy in her life is that she got to Harvard and Princeton twenty years too late. What she would give to have been part of the beautiful sexual free-for-all that flourished at Harvard in the late sixties and early seventies!

But when I read her description of Harvard as she thinks it was during the time I was there – I think: Who sold her *that* story? While I cannot find a single point of comparison between her prelapsarian fantasies and the miseries my friends and I endured in the name of sexual experimentation, I do find all too many points of reference in her gloomy descriptions of Harvard night life. That party she describes in which all the women pulled off their blouses to put on a brave front of liberation while 'dancing to the rhythm of frustration'[29] I remember it well, except that my memory is *circa* 1972. That cutting remark about her feminist classmates being ideologically opposed to men but wanting them anyway[30] – she thinks this is a new phenomenon? It is not feminist ambivalence we are looking at here, it is puritan ambivalence dressed in feminist language. It ought to be too obvious to mention that this is ambivalence that has plagued Harvard students since the very beginning just as it has plagued the entire country since the very beginning.

And what makes Katie Roiphe think she's an exception? Even as she rails against puritanism, and extols the virtues of the polymorphously perverse, she fights her fight using puritan archetypes. She describes Catharine MacKinnon and her cohorts as witches who have sullied the pure feminism she acquired from her mother.[31]

If I think of MacKinnon in the same way, it's because I have a puritan streak too. Which is why I have a soft spot for Paglia, who flaunts her hatred for all things puritan and so breaks the spell. Unfortunately, she doesn't have a soft spot for people like me. This is the Paglia Position on breeders:

> ... Feminism was always wrong to pretend that women could have it all. It is not male society but mother nature who lays the heaviest burden on women. No husband or daycare centre can ever adequately substitute for a mother's attention. My feminist models are the boldly independent Amelia Earhart and Katharine Hepburn, who has been outspoken in her opposition to the delusion of 'having it all'.[32]

Thanks a billion, Camille. I appreciate your concern. I do not think, therefore I *am* a mother. Eh?

I particularly like the way she waives our civil rights on account of our being powerful enough already. And better than institutionalised care, no less! Better even than fathers! Wow! Where will all this power get us?

Not very far, the prophetess assures us: 'Women must take personal responsibility for the path they have chosen and stop whining about the options they have thereby lost.' It ought to be satisfaction enough to see our children thriving. 'There is nothing more important than motherhood – not because it is "care-giving" but because it is the primal source of all life and contains its own dark, ambiguous dualities.'[33]

In other words, we are to keep our mouths shut. Be content with our dualities. Revel in the knowledge that we loom over the collective unconscious like so many nuclear deterrents. Leave the thinking and acting and exploring to your Amelias, your Katharines, and your Camilles. And stay out of feminism! 'A feminism that canonises itself as unconditional love just turns itself into a big udder for hating and hateful people.'[34]

The problem with lesbians, she goes on to say, is that they never manage to separate from their mothers. They could, if they bothered, learn an awful lot from men: 'Every man must define his identity against his mother. If he does not, he just falls back into her and is swallowed up.' Gay men forge their independence by having anonymous sex, she says, while men who go to prostitutes are 'valiantly striving to keep sex free from emotion, duty, family – in other words from society, religion, and procreative Mother Nature'.[35]

And if you think: Oh well, Camille would say that, wouldn't she – then find me the feminist classic that doesn't echo this scenario in some way, that isn't striving to contain the great powers of Mother, or more to the point, Mother Nature. Books for the general feminist public that give mothers any degree of sympathetic treatment go to extreme lengths to identify them first as victims of male chauvinist warriors (as Phyllis Chesler and Marilyn French do) or as paragons of virtue and significance who need to be preserved in their traditional ruts (as Selma Fraiberg did when she wrote *In Defence of Mothering*) or as redundant objects to be pitied as they cede centre stage to their offspring (as Nancy Friday did in another book with a title that says it all, *My Mother My Self*).

It seems important, also, to affirm that procreation and lust have nothing to do with each other, that the erotic is only erotic if the shadow of the mother has been thoroughly erased. A recent French theory-inspired feminist encyclopaedia called *The Sexual Imagination* had an entry for 'phallus' but not for 'womb', for 'menopause' but not for 'menarche' or 'menses'. It did not even have an entry for 'fertility goddess'!

You think this was a simple case of oversight? Allow me to rob you of your innocence. Let me introduce you to Donna J. Haraway, one of the most imaginative thinkers of academic feminism. She began her professional life, in her own words, as 'a proper US socialist-feminist, white, female, hominid biologist'. She now calls herself a cyborg feminist. She thinks we're all cyborgs now because our identities have merged with our computers. She thinks that the only hope for women is to take this merger to its logical limit. If we can really really really merge with our machines, then we will no longer be beholden in the way that we are now to our mothers and fathers. We won't be born innocent any more. We'll begin life gloriously genderless and with a full computer database. This means we won't need to suffer through childhood, and so won't need families. Saved from the ills of domestic patriarchy, free of all those stupid myths about the Garden of Eden and the fall from innocence, from day one we'll be too hip to fall for the lies of patriarchal politics. We'll devote our lives to playing computer wars with Dr Strangelove.[36]

Haraway insists that her Utopian vision is ironic. I agree with her. I find it very ironic indeed that she and her fellow cyborg feminists have put so much effort into imagining futures where we no longer need to have or become mothers. Far be it for me to suggest they're wasting their time. Family-free Utopias satisfy a need that active, real-world feminism cannot meet. This is the need not to grow up.

Haraway says Utopias are not so much blueprints for the future but maps of our souls. Her own map suggests a movement dominated by rich girls and child-free academics who are frozen inside the fears and resentments they have been carrying around with them since they turned eighteen. A movement of Lost Girls who are so determined not to do anything that might turn them into their mothers that they can't even bear to think about maternity.

Or should I have said a *cult* of Lost Girls? You could argue that that is where the current trend is leading – to a cult that holds its moral power by keeping its priestesses child-free and separate, and by urging the rest of us to search and then research the treachery in our own hearts. That teaches us to control and police and mistrust our natural urges. That complains rather smugly, and rather like the Church, about falling attendance. That makes any woman who consorts with patriarchs feel as if she is breaking all ten commandments. That has been so keen to sever the link between that fascinating, elusive concept, sexuality, and its correspondent, ooey-gooey, disgusting procreation, and so poetic in its redefinitions, which are themselves ever more distant from ooey-gooey and possibly virus-ridden bodily fluids, that a Martian could easily assume sexuality was the modern term for spirituality.

Why do they hate us so much?

Maybe it's because of these books we read. This torture we subject ourselves to, even pay good money for. I am talking about the feminist literature addressed specifically to mothers. Our capitulation is illustrated on every cover. What a collection of options you never wanted!

Let me try and count them as I hurl them into the bin. Let's see, first to go are those grim tomes about how good mothers are and how badly we're getting treated and how society and feminism better get more caring, or else! *The War Against Mothers. Prisoners of Men's Dreams*. Their titles are enough to make you want to suffocate yourself with your pillow. They name the enemy, but never get around to telling you how to win, do they? All they do is add another layer to your despair. Although that is preferable, don't you think, to the ones that tell you what a bad job you've done simply because there is something wrong with your unconscious.

Their titles say it all, too. *The Bonds of Love*. *Jocasta's Children*. They might well have called them *There is No Hope for Improvement*. The most depressing of the lot, because it is written by a working mother and based on indepth interviews with working mothers, is Ros Coward's *Our Treacherous Hearts*. She argues that we have become mothers in order to hide from the real world. We are inadvertently training our daughters to be weaklings, and our sons oppressors. And if we give up our place in the working world to do this bad job more thoroughly, our personal decisions have social consequences. The possibility of collective action becomes more remote each time one of us capitulates.

How to atone for our sins? There is only one option. We must get men involved. What if they won't? The evil-unconscious brigade remain ominously silent on this one. Unfortunately, there is another subsubgenre to offer solace in the place of solutions. I am talking now about the books that aim to enrich your birth experience, or mend the Cartesian split – finally! After so many centuries of discomfort! – by getting you back in harmony with your body, or trace your motherline back to the Egyptians, or find the goddess within you, all in the comfort of your very own gilded cage.

Although at least they leave you, the mother, in charge of the cage. At least they want to make you happy. The same cannot be said of the practical books for working mothers. When you consider that there are some very good books out there criticising and even deriding patriarchal efforts to control women with advice books – for example, Barbara Ehrenreich and Deirdre English's *For Her Own Good: Fifty Years of the Experts' Advice to Women*; and Christina Hardyment's *Dream Babies* – it is shocking to read what feminists have so far offered in their place.

Least objectionable, but very, very depressing because so very, very realistic, are the manuals like *Working Mother*. Its authors resent the amount of coping their target readers have to do, but they see no way forward except to help them cope better. 'We offer all our support and good wishes to those of you who can change ... your own home,' they say between clenched teeth, 'and we believe that more of us can and will do so. But meanwhile there is the ironing to be done.'[37]

Of course you know that they know that you are a martyr. Negative thoughts like this are just not tolerated, though, in the more aggressive feminist-childcare, husband-and-career-managing books. These begin from the premise that human liberation is a question of mental equilibrium and efficiency.[38]

Ban dolls! say the bring-up-your-child-sex-blind brigade. Spend some time on yourself or else! cry the relaxation experts: after thirty minutes of exercise you have no choice but to close your eyes while lying on your side on your mat for exactly seven seconds! 'The ancients called the desert a place of divine revelation,' announces Clarissa Pinkola Estes. 'But, for women, there is much more to it than that.'[39]

I couldn't have said it better myself. I think I'll make it into a poster and hang it on my refrigerator. The one I'm going to burn ritualistically is a book called *Juggling* by Faye J. Crosby, a psychologist who teaches at Betty Friedan's alma mater, Smith.

She is aware that our problems have social and political dimensions, but reminds us 'that the need for collective action does not cancel out the need for individual action'.[40] The way forward is to lessen stress by 'cognitive reframing – that is, rethinking realities'. What we need to do is visualise ourselves as jugglers – imagine each 'life role' as an Indian club, and then focus on each one in our mind's eye, and ask how fragile or sturdy it is, if it's beautiful or ugly or difficult to catch, how it feels to toss or grasp. 'Is its flight path predictable and smooth or wobbly and uncertain?' she asks disingenuously. 'Does it exert any gravitational pull on any of the other clubs? How would I feel if it were harmed? Broken or dented?'

> The more concrete the question, the better. [Once a woman] has fixed a quite detailed image of each separate item in her mind and has used these images to illuminate distinctions, she is ready to conjure up images of action. She should watch the internal movie of herself juggling all the clubs to see when she feels happy and satisfied and when she feels worried. She could see then how she attends to the children, to her job, to

her friends. [And, if she really went all the way, she could] use metaphor analysis to help reduce the stress of juggling without minimalising the pleasures of balancing different life roles. She would gain the composure that comes from knowing she is prepared for any emergency. And she would lose none of the fun of combining roles.[41]

The point I'm trying to make is not that this sort of advice is ridiculous but that it is the only type of advice there is! All the more depressing, then, that she makes it sound as if we are court jesters who are attending the Lord's banquet on sufferance. Performing our desperate best to make sure we get asked back. It implies that everywhere we go we are X personally responsible for absolutely everything. And are in constant danger of alienating the stray good men who might help us. We really have to watch how and where we vent our generalised anger about the unfairness of it all: anger will get you nowhere, she reminds us.[42] What we need to do is what mothers have always done, which is hold our tongues and step back and try to see the problem through everyone's eyes but our own.

It all comes down to the same simple message: stand on the margin and SMILE!

She would like us to take *especial* care with the feelings of these men who aren't helping us enough. The way Faye J. Crosby sees it, they're doing what you and I would have done in their position – clinging to old privileges. Not because they're malicious, but because they're insensitive and short-sighted. 'When men put on aprons, they incur several immediate losses.' They include: loss of breadwinner status, loss of unpaid assistant in the course of their careers, loss of intimacy due to crazy schedules, and loss of authority due to their economically autonomous wives having greater say. Because anyone facing these prospects will prove 'resistant to change', any working mother who wants to share the juggling equitably had better approach him with empathy, tact, and gentle persuasion.[43] The circus metaphor this brings to mind is lion-taming without a whip.

Or ironing without an iron.

But we are looking at a problem larger than laundry. This ought to be obvious. So why isn't it? Why are the few feminist thinkers who address the problem of the working woman's double load so stuck in logistics? Why so much attention on the man who needs to be trained, the employer who needs to be enlightened? Why so little attention to the larger picture? Why is it the working mother, the person in the picture who is stretched closest to her outer limit, who is now supposed to mastermind and engineer the domestic revolution *and* reshape the work culture? Why do writers who call themselves feminists persist in thinking that these poor creatures can win freedom, liberty and justice for all, as well as pursue their own happiness, simply by becoming more efficient?

Why do we put up with it? What is it that makes it so hard for us to speak out on our own behalf? Why do we let other feminists talk for us, and down to us, and over our heads?

2

THE NAMELESS HORROR

I can only speak for myself

Or more to the point, I can't. From the fateful morning in November 1970 when I picked up Kate Millett off the bathroom floor of a house where I was babysitting, and discovered that my idol, D. H. Lawrence, was a sadistic woman-hater, I was in awe of these radicalised headmistresses who got the second wave rolling – in awe of their certainty and in awe of their indisputably wider experience. They saw it all, suffered it all first. Large tragedies littered their lives. They had been chained to kitchens, reduced to housekeeping machines, denied educations, beaten by sexists, yoked by motherhood, and then, indignity of all indignities, when they finally identified the problem with no name, and dragged themselves out of their ruts, and struggled through divorces and child-custody battles so as to win the right to a decent education – where did they end up, but in a classroom presided over by another brute who told them D. H. Lawrence was a genius! What could I – or any other overprivileged snot my age – hope to offer to match such hard-luck stories? We knew better than to try. And so, for the most part, we did as we were told. We shut up, and listened, and promised to make full and grateful use of the advantages they had won for us. We exchanged one set of matriarchs for another at the age of eighteen. Twenty-five years later, this league of altermaters is still in charge of my head.

And if I say these women remind me of my mother, I hope you understand that I do not mean my real mother, who told me to beware of typing skills, who forgot to show me how to make a bed. Who was so keen for us to see the world that she thought nothing of drying my younger brother's nappies on the pyramids. Who is always saying try it, you'll like it, do it, you'll be fine, buy it, you deserve it, give them hell, they deserve it, and congratulations, you've done well. No. I'm talking about the mother who lives inside my head, who tells me I'm never good enough, and that my most altruistic acts are secretly self-serving, and that, even at the age of forty-two, I'm still a slut. Who implies, with silent reproachful eyes, that I have been her ruination since the moment of my birth. Who is never fooled. Who always knows better. Who threatens wordlessly to arrange for the earth to swallow me up should I have the temerity to cross her. Who implies, again wordlessly, that one word of criticism from me will have the destructive force of a ton of bricks. Who makes men look easy.

I know these feelings are infantile and even primitive. Knowing this hasn't changed much. I am still unable to address mother figures as equals. No, it's even worse. I find myself unable to vent a single disrespectful word in their presence. The thought forms, the words prepare to roll off my tongue, and then, whoosh, they're gone. Let me give you an example. Six or seven years ago, I got an assignment to interview Marilyn French, who was in town to promote her new blockbuster about three generations of strong, deeply depressing women. I was myself very keen to meet her, first because I had convinced myself I hated everything she stood for, and second because we had been at Harvard, and in the same department, at the same time. When I had first picked up *The Women's Room*, I had recognised in the author's photo one of the grim faces that had haunted me in the library stacks, and convinced me by their cautionary example to stay away from graduate school.

Today, as I watched her amble across the foyer of Claridge's, she looked an infinitely more stylish woman. Bejewelled, dressed in expensive silks, she was carefully courteous as she directed me into the dining room where a table was waiting for us. I put my new tape recorder on the table and clicked it on. With motherly tact, she said, 'Don't you think you'd prefer to wait until after we've ordered?' After we had ordered, she said, 'Are you sure you're going to be able to pick up my voice if you have the microphone under that napkin?' She guided me through the question-and-answer routine as you might guide a disgruntled child through a tricky bit of long division.

This was annoying as I found her ideas as pat as ever. She told me, among other things, that every mother chose one daughter to whom to pass on her secret sorrows. How about the ones who only had sons? I wanted but did not dare to ask. Instead, I asked her what role men had to play in childrearing. 'No one should ever count on them,' she said firmly. 'I'm not against men. Don't get me wrong. They can be fun as playmates. But expect them to help with the children, and they'll let you down. Anyway, who wants them helping out? Who needs them? Let them go hunting. It's a much better idea to establish a network with other women. After all, that's what women did before patriarchy.'

What a load of rubbish, I thought to myself. This woman has no idea how people my age live, and yet here she is presuming to tell us what to do, and then justifying her arguments with bogus anthropology. 'How can you be so sure?' I blurted out. And then, I stopped, aghast at my brazenness.

'*Well*,' she said. She gave me a long, sad, searching, but at the same time knowing, look. 'I can tell,' she said, as she took a long, elegant drag from her long, brown cigarette. 'I can tell you that there is one person at this table who hasn't read my book on women and power!'

My voice rose into a panic-stricken tweet. 'No! I know! I haven't. Not yet! But I plan to! Before I write up this interview!'

She gave me a second long, reproving, but faintly amused stare, then reached out and put a calming hand on my arm. 'Don't worry,' she said. 'Everything is going to be fine. Here,' she said. 'You look like you're still hungry. Why don't you have some of my salad?'

I hated her! More than ever! She was wrong, and I was right, but she had won the argument by pulling rank on me. By being *nice*! It wasn't fair, I thought, as my best manners reasserted themselves against my will. Yes, I heard myself saying. I'd love to eat your salad. And I did, and while I did, she asked me about my work and my children, and my soon-to-be ex-husband and listened to my shameless sob story with concerned interest, and gave me advice that was, while not particularly imaginative, certainly sensible. Then, to make matters worse, she told me about her own daughter's recent rape.

This woman trusted me. How guilty I felt as I thanked her for giving me her time! A month later, when the magazine I was working for folded, my one source of relief was that I was not going to have to betray her by airing my dirty laundry of disloyal opinions in public.

But the tape remains, and it betrays *me*.

My case against the Lost Girls is that they've locked us all into adolescence. The sad fact is that I am locked into another variation of the same thing, along with the rest of my generation, even those of us who have gone on to have our own children. We're contained in a sullen simmering silence, because to speak is disloyal and destructive, while also, paradoxically, futile. But now, as we simmer silently, we are in danger of losing the privileged status that made our suffering bearable. Until recently, we had only one generation overlooking us, and we could afford to feel young, abandoned, morally superior in a way there was no need to define. Now, because of this new generation of younger feminists, who ignore our existence in a supercilious way that is all too familiar, we're finding ourselves not so much overlooked as boxed in.

See if this rings any bells with you. I was trying on a new dress for the benefit of a friend. It was a dress both she and I liked because it was the sort of thing our mothers would never have dreamed of wearing at our age. My ten-year-old daughter liked it, too. She asked if I could save it for her so that she could wear it when she was older.

'Oh, I remember I used to ask my mother that,' said my friend. 'And you know what the worst thing was? She did.'

My friend and I laughed. My daughter didn't get the joke. I told her she would come to understand it only too well, especially if I kept my promise to her.

'But I want the dress!' she insisted.

'You won't when you're big enough to fit into it.'

'How do you know?'

'I just do.'

'I can't stand it,' she said. 'You think you even know how I'll feel when I grow up. You can't know *everything*! It's just not fair.' As she stormed out of the room, I smiled again, but as I was turning to my friend, I caught a glimpse of the mirror. And there she was. The image of my mother, smiling just as superciliously, but at me.

And that just about sums it up. That's where I find myself, no matter where I go – caught between the mother in the mirror who knows me better than I know myself, and the daughter who wants to run away from me because I know why she'll never want to wear my dress. The mother who sees through me. The daughter who can't bear to look.

I see the same pattern inside the women's movement, as women fifteen years older than I shout over my head at women who are fifteen years younger. I suppose I should say oh well, it's really so predictable. The Greeks already wrote about it. There are things about mothers and daughters that you've just got to accept. But something in me says no, there's more to life than frozen classical poses. If we remain fixed in these poses, and resigned about them as well as fixed, we can't even hope for anything better. If we're ever going to break out of those poses, we need to understand why it's so difficult for mothers, and feminists, to speak openly and be heard by daughters, and younger feminists. We need to look very carefully at the silences, not just to appreciate the nurturing they make possible and the peace they preserve, but also to understand the wisdom that does not get passed on in the name of nurturing and the problems that do not get worked out in the name of peacekeeping.

We need feminists to look at the feminist legacy in the same spirit of critical enquiry we are always urging men to adopt when they look at the legacy of patriarchy. We need to seek out the contradictions, and try to understand them, instead of evading and escaping them. Most of all, we need to look at the tangle of myths and primitive fears inside feminist ideas about motherhood – not just because four-fifths of women do become mothers, but because the patterns of this mysterious, largely unarticulated, female-only legacy echo so insistently in the history of feminism.

But talk about taboos. Talk about unpopular subjects. There is no faster way to get up mainstream feminists' noses

And if you don't believe me, try yourself. Try standing up in front of a group of child-free feminists – they can even be any age, they can even be friends – and say, actually, there is something to be said in favour of mothers. Say I can understand why it's a touchy subject, historically speaking, and I know that it can slow a woman down, or lower her into avoidable servitude, but even so, mothers make an important contribution and we shouldn't rush to throw the whole concept out of the window. Say this, and what do you get? A room full of women with their hands over their ears. Here are a few of the slurs you can expect if you persist:

Fifties throwback, maternal revivalist, elitist, ethnocentrist. And worst of all, essentialist. This is a term coined by Elizabeth V. Spelman.[1] It's what you are if you assume that there are any attributes common to all women. (The standards drop slightly if you are assigning attributes to all men.) The worst kind of essentialist is the one who is educated, middle class, white, and assumes that any problem she has is shared by all females worldwide, and who, likewise, assumes that any problems these other women have, that she doesn't have, aren't really that important. I live in constant danger of turning into this kind of essentialist.

But then again, I would have this problem even if I were not educated, middle class, white, and articulate. It is very hard to speak about the problems common to mothers without coming dangerously close to describing essences. This is a risk even if you are very careful, and describe not what mothers are, but what they do, and what they become because they do. Even if you are aware of the evil that is essentialism, and phrase your words so as not to offend, the central idea – that mothers are worthy of help and attention – remains mysteriously elusive.

This is so even when you are denouncing essentialism. Take bell hooks, an African-American feminist who has argued passionately that motherhood is not just central to the experience of black women, but far preferable to the degrading and dehumanising work they have had to do from slavery up until the present. She accuses middle-class, college-educated white feminists of assuming their own views of motherhood to be universal.[2] Her accusations have been taken very, very seriously by white, middle-class, feminist academics – but only as a warning about racism, and not as yet another instance of prejudice against mothers. No one has stood up in public and asked: What similarities are there between the mothers bell hooks describes and the mothers in other classes or cultures? Is there anything other mothers can learn from bell hooks' mothers? What does she know about ourselves as mothers that we don't know? No one has asked these questions because to ask them would be to break the rules of the essentialist game. The rules say that bell hooks has *carte blanche* to say what she wants so long as she keeps to her own category.

And so, while the threat of essentialism sometimes puts a curb on racism, it does not put a curb on anti-maternalism. The two fastest ways for an anti-maternalist feminist to combat a pro-maternalist statement is either to denounce it as essentialist – or to say that it only applies to the category to which the speaker belongs. The easiest way to avoid such a dismissal is to downplay the importance of what you're trying to say, to couch it in so many qualifications that it ceases to mean anything, or to return to that most traditional of sacred vows, maternal silence.

Which you could dismiss as simple courtesy, or even as a variant of affirmative action to equalise the power imbalance between mothers and daughters, were it not for the way this maternal silence has helped to hide a contradiction at the heart of feminist thought:

Modern feminists like to see themselves as adventurers, daring to look beyond the convenient façades of patriarchy to stare the truth in the face. Daring to say the unsayable. Making the private public so as to hold the public accountable. As a consequence, there has been a lot of earnest discussion over the past twenty-five years about women's historical silence and the importance of listening to women's voices. On the tragic side of the chorus we've had Tillie Olsen sobbing at the ironing board about all the books that were born in her heart only to die unwritten while she was raising all those children. On the heroic side we've had Toni Morrison and Margaret Atwood not just conjuring voices to the surface but daring to explore their ironies and so turning them into art.

Then we've had the thousands and thousands of feminist academics chipping away at the foundations of the ivory towers that house and feed them. Some, like Carol Gilligan, write to a mass audience. Others, like Julia Kristeva, address only a deconstructed elite. *All* use women's testimony, women's experience, women's marginalised wisdom to call into question our most cherished manmade assumptions about separation, independence and autonomy; public and private values; nature and culture; paid and unpaid work; right, wrong relationships and connection; the certainties of the scientific method; the assumptions of psychology, linguistics, sociology, anthropology, history, economics, philosophy, politics. Not to mention religion. The humanities. Power. Love. The meaning of life. Very little is sacred. Despite vast areas of disagreement, and incompatible styles, the refrain remains radically constant: the history of man is at best only half the story. The full story shows that the old story existed primarily to justify the primacy of a chosen few. If the general public ever read this stuff and took its findings seriously, civilization as we know it would end tomorrow.

As things stand now, the literature of feminist subversion doesn't even reach most academics. But the best work seeps through, and this is especially true of the work that remains formally within the disciplines it is questioning. It would be hard to think of a body of thought that feminist writers haven't seriously undermined, but it is not hard to see why this would be so, as the most challenging work has always come from thinkers and artists and writers who are in the uncomfortable but intellectually privileged position of having to work both within a tradition and outside it.

But this same privilege has created serious political problems for the feminist movement itself. If facts are not *really* facts but value statements, if all ideologies are based on beautiful lies, what is there left to go on? How to protect your own values and articles of faith from your own corrosive X-ray vision? How to act with conviction? How to identify what all the different schools of feminism have in common? How to decide what is right and what is wrong and how to learn from mistakes? When to doubt? When to go on gut feeling? Can you understand why you believe in something and still believe it? Can you figure out what makes a movement tick, or not tick, without dismantling it? The anthropologist Emily Martin calls this problem 'trying to push a bus in which you are riding'.[3]

When you're trying to push the bus you're in, barbs intended for patriarchs have a way of turning into boomerangs. Having exposed the self-serving lies of patriarchal elites, you can't help wondering about the feminist elite. What are *its* self-serving lies? Just how democratic and pluralistic is it? How many women can it claim to speak for? It might be listening to lots of voices, it might be respectful of diversity, but how much is it distorting, and when it does distort, what secret ideological agenda is it seeking to justify? British feminists, French feminists, African, Asian, and Latin American feminists, minority feminists, radical feminists, socialist feminists, Lacanian feminists, Marxist Freudian feminists, Foucault-inspired postmodern feminists – just about all feminists, in fact, who do not happen to be the white and bright products of Oxbridge and Ivy League educations have been vociferous and eloquent about their (I suppose I should in all honesty say 'our') tendency to repeat the original sin: condemning the oppressed to silence by presuming to speak for them. Recent feminist academic writing is full of nervous, apologetic tributes to previously misdefined and passed over feminists of colour. The driving force behind feminist postmodernism has been to move beyond, and if necessary, destroy, the movement's monocultural beginnings to celebrate instead the rich rainbow quilt that is Women's Experience.

But there are problems in this programme. The first is the fragility of the coalition. It lacks a centre. It lives in a bunker designed for its windows and its criticial viewpoint. At times it seems held together only by its collective ambivalence about its foundations – its much eroded but still suspect elitist grounding. (Without which none of these academic feminists could hope to live.) The second is the fierceness of the general female opposition to feminism – and the fact that much of the opposition comes from the poor, uneducated, culturally opiated mothers our rainbow chorus would most like to liberate. No one wants to talk down to them, or dismiss them. That would be positively patriarchal. At the same time, no one wants to admit them to the symposium: that would be movement suicide.

So survival depends on the ritualistic celebration of a common myth – an inspiring variation on Beauty and the Beast – as well as the observance of an unspoken etiquette. This involves a stoical open-arms policy *vis-à-vis* the exploited unconvinced (except occasionally when they have fired the first shot) and a respectful muteness in the face of criticism from feminists who can claim to be doubly or triply oppressed by virtue of their race, class, and/or nationality. And (partly because this involves much strain and more tact) it is also understood that there are certain feminist assumptions that must not be subjected to the trial of doubt or even in-house enquiry.

Motherhood, especially motherhood as experienced by white, middle-class, educated and ethnocentric women with essentialist tendencies, is the taboo topic to end all taboo topics because it combines so many. At its most significant cultural moment, birth, it requires a man or a doctor, or both, and so raises questions about purity. Before, during, and after birth, it implies, even though it need not involve a desire for men and a dependence on doctors, and so raises questions about autonomy. Because patriarchy could not exist without mothers, anyone who becomes a mother is colluding with patriarchy. *Reproducing* patriarchy.

There are feminists who have challenged these suspicions. But they never come out and denounce them as anti-maternal prejudices. Instead, they bite their nails, worry that their sisters might walk out of the symposium before they get to the point! There are times when they treat even their own ideas like potential traitors.

Take Jessica Benjamin, the author of *The Bonds of Love*, a psychological re-examination of early psychic life that treats babies and their mothers as equally important, and that proposes their relationship is not based on domination and subjugation but mutual recognition. Underpinning her beautiful descriptions of mothers interacting with babies is the premise that there is something of value, something worth preserving and even developing, in traditional mothering. Instead of critiquing those feminist writers who have so insistently suggested otherwise, she goes out of her way to thank them for the work they have done in demystifying that evil, traditional motherhood – and then denounces as 'gender conservatives' feminists who come and say what she herself has implied – that there are a few aspects of families and traditional motherhood worth saving. You get the feeling she is flailing herself to prove her feminist loyalties – or terrified of the trap her own ideas might lead her into.

Mary O'Brien is more level-headed but just as fearful of her audience. This despite her project, which could not be bolder: to rewrite the political account, from Plato to Marx. She believes that the entire tradition of Western philosophy originates from a male sense of exclusion from birth and genetic continuity, and is an attempt to compensate for these bitter facts of life by providing a space for men only. In *The Politics of Reproduction*, she makes a brave attempt to base a philosophy for women on the new facts of life as altered by technology. This is in sharp contrast to what so many others have done, which is to grow a philosophy for women out of cuttings from old philosophies for men. (As Simone de Beauvoir did with existentialism, Betty Friedan with liberalism, Shulamith Firestone and Kate Millett with Marxism, and even Juliet Mitchell with Freud.)

But her daring is only skin deep. After eight pages of rousing let's-storm-the-Bastille-type rhetoric, she suddenly loses her nerve and admits: 'I can no longer withhold the information that this book is really about motherhood: despised, derided and neglected motherhood.'[4] You can almost see her cringe over her typewriter, almost hear her imaginary audience crying, 'What a bummer!' Which is more or less what it did.

Another martyr to the cause: the feminist philosopher, Sara Ruddick, who wrote a rigorously argued and desperately eager-to-please book entitled *Maternal Thinking*. Its earth-shaking thesis is that mothering requires intelligence. Mothers have to think, says Sara Ruddick, because even their most basic duties – to protect, nurture, and train their children – are forever in conflict. The doubt that stems from this endless string of tricky judgements makes mothers reflective about the work they do. This means that they are not just mechanically meeting children's needs, as so many experts claim. Neither are they brainlessly passing on cultural values determined by their elders and betters. When they share their doubts and develop their theories with other mothers (and fathers, and carers), what they are doing is engaging in their own peculiar form of disciplined discourse. To anyone who has looked after children, this makes perfect sense. It combines well with the premise, best expressed by Jean Bethke Elshtain,[5] and acted upon in small, noble ways by Ann Oakley and other feminist sociologists, that feminine tradition is worth exploring and preserving, at least in part. But it remains mysteriously controversial in feminist circles.[6]

Sara Ruddick discovered this when she went out to present her ideas to the general public and the feminist faithful. As she confesses in her beautifully diplomatic way:

> Sometimes it has been difficult to present – even as a lively hypothesis for collective reflection – the idea that a distinctive kind of thinking arises from the work of mothers. Frequently questioners will be quite explicit. The idea of maternity is sentimental and reactionary. 'Talking about mothers leaves me out.' (Said by women and men.) More often, these people express an unease I cannot name.[7]

I know how she feels, but let's give it a try anyhow. Let's start by admitting that there are lots of reasons, political, social, cultural and emotional, why feminists might be suspicious of motherhood. The word can't help but have a prim, joyless, conservative ring to it. As does maternal thinking. And practice. Even if you are wary of tradition, motherhood has a way of drawing you into it. There is no way of remaining on the cynical margin, and almost no way of steering clear of patriarchal social pressure.

Having a child is the fastest way of turning into a second-class citizen – and yet it is something that most women still want and actively choose. Why? The acceptable answer for elitist feminists who presume to speak for the teeming multitudes is that most women have no other route to status and fulfilment.

Where this is clearly not the case, no excuse is fully acceptable.[8] So if you are a woman who has had children even though you had better options, you simply do not make sense to orthodox child-free feminists. If you add to the annoying mystery by complaining that you don't have it easy, impatience turns to antipathy.

What to do when you're speaking to someone who doesn't want to hear you? The humane, maternal response to the problem of feminist antipathy to maternity is the same as to the problem of male antipathy to maternity. It is to stand in the prejudiced person's shoes and seek to understand her. In other words, to be motherly. To make allowances. To wait until the right time comes up to suggest the same idea in different, more attractive garb. To hold your tongue. To appease, if only for the time being. To couch all pro-maternal thoughts in careful language, and never ever ever to go on the offensive. Hope instead that one day the great feminist thinkers of the world will wake up and appreciate our worth. Except that this leads to the same outcome as all other appeasements. My story, our story, falls through the gap. My, our experiences are denied. My, our view of things grossly misrepresented in another's voice. The reasons for the fear of us remain unexplored, and so the fear is fanned.

It is through well-meaning silence that mothers become the Others of feminism – in much the same way that women became the Others of patriarchy. Which can't be right. Which has to be a betrayal of everything feminism was supposed to be about. Which would indicate that the only way forward is to speak about motherhood publicly.

Although this presents serious problems.

Let me try and explain what I mean without presuming to speak for anyone but myself.

I'll begin by standing you outside my house

Big, isn't it? Beautiful, too – wouldn't you say? That gate – it's like something out of Transylvania. It would be easy to jump to conclusions but don't. The house is not ours. The rent is bankrupting us. Why are we here, then? Because it's the right size. Because I find I work better in congenial surroundings. And because I have no money sense.

Unless it's a question of something I didn't want to buy in the first place. One thing you won't find as you make your way to the front door is a car large enough to hold all eight of us. Frank thinks – with some justice – that I ought to be the one to buy this. I think – with just as much justice – that we ought to buy it jointly. As the disagreement drags into its fourth year, we continue to drive the two very old cars we had before we set up house together, each of us praying that the other one's car will be the one to pack up first.

Do not assume too much from this failure to co-operate. Come into the kitchen first and watch us do breakfast. The man sitting at the table stoically contemplating yesterday's paper – that's Frank. He's in charge of Helen, the three year old, and Pandora, the toddler, while I take a shower. He may not appear to be watching them, but look, look! The moment Pandora notices an open door and makes for the stairs, he's up and after her! That might not sound like much, but I bet you can think of five men you know who wouldn't have even noticed.

Let me introduce you to the others. The boy making two packed lunches at the counter – that's Kimber, Frank's thirteen-year-old son from his first marriage. The large-eyed girl pouring out cereal for the toddler – that's Rachel, his ten-year-old daughter. That pouting creature sitting half-dressed and half-asleep by the Aga – that's my eleven-year-old daughter Emma. That hulk who is ironing his school shirt – that's Matthew, my sixteen-year-old son, also from my first marriage. All this talk of first marriages might lead you to think that these exist in opposition to some second marriage. In fact, Frank and I are not married.

Is this a sign of independence on my part (or his part, or our part) or is it a sign of indecision? Am I left with not enough security as a result, or not enough power? Is it fair that Frank has no paternal rights unless we do marry? If this is his main reason for wanting to marry, might I be wise to resist? Was it right, or stupid, or perverse to give our two children his last name instead of mine? You could argue about it for ever, which is why I'd like to ask you to move quickly over this patch of feminist quicksand and instead give me my due for getting my son to take charge of his grooming. Don't look too closely, or you'll see he's failed to unroll his shirt-sleeves. Having passed the iron briefly over the body of the shirt, he puts it on as is. Carefully, he sets the iron on top of the microwave. This is to keep it out of the baby's reach. Don't worry about his having forgotten to unplug the thing. Because those are my shoes you hear clicking so self-importantly down the stairs. The first thing you'll see me do when I get to the kitchen is check the iron. Do I do this because I have lower expectations of boys when it comes to electrical appliances? And if so, does this mean I am indulging or undermining him? Reinforcing or correcting his already worrying supremacist views? Please feel free to explore these issues. Anything but pay too much attention to my clothes.

Frank *does* notice my clothes. This is close to being out of character. 'Is that a suede jacket?' he asks. I attempt a preoccupied nod, but he persists. 'Is it new?' 'No,' I say. 'I've had it for ages.' This is a lie. Although I have no reason to lie. For God's sake, it's my money, isn't it? Anyway, looking after my appearance is important! If I don't, I won't get any work. Will I? So it's not just vanity! So don't even try to give me that pursuit-of-eternal-youth-and-beauty-myth crap. I'm a grown woman! I'll wear what I like!

But what does the original lie to Frank say about our relationship? My character? The degree to which I have managed to alter my gendered consciousness? Twenty-five years of lectures, and I'm still compulsively buying clothes I can't afford? I would of course be overjoyed if you insisted that it isn't my fault on account of my gendered consciousness having been structured by people who didn't know any better before I myself knew how to speak.

I'll buy *that* lie at any price. Not that it matters as Frank is no longer with us. He's gone out to the Transylvanian gate to get the post and today's paper. You will notice, I'm sure, that when he gets back there will not be any question as to who gets to read the first section first. This may or may not speak volumes about the division of work and privilege in our household. Even if it does, it may not be the whole story. Because, look, he's already telling me about an article on page 7 that will interest me. And now he's standing up to get me a book he brought home for me from the office. It's not as if we live in two separate worlds! I'll read the paper! But don't rush me! I'll read it later, after I've made the grocery list.

Running the house is my job, but even this duty is not clear-cut, because I delegate. Today, as on every weekday, the nanny is doing the shopping, and even though I'm supposed to cook on weekdays, today Frank is cooking because I'm spending the day in London and won't be back till seven.

Do you want to know why I'm going to London? It's rather interesting, and rather important. Oh, I see, I should have guessed. You'd prefer to know how I justify a nanny. I'll spare you my usual storm of half-excuses because they don't even convince me. And I'll spare you (but only for the time being) the sob stories about uncertified but certifiable babysitters, nightmarish daycare centres, and melodramas I, or rather, my children, endured before I went deluxe. In exchange for this favour, I would greatly appeciate it if you would not remind me how ironic it is that in order to liberate myself I have to exploit another woman.

I do try and pay her as much as I can! Even though I'm pretty sure she would not see it the same way! And I let her know how much I value her work, even though she'd make a lot more money doing just about anything else! Does it help to know I used to do this job? Does that give some weight to my claim that a few years in a job like this can be a helpful link between school and adulthood?

Tell me some other time, because here she is now to take the children to school and me to the train. She's come forty-five minutes earlier than usual. She's wonderfully flexible as well as reliable. I don't know what I'd do without her – even though it does occur to me from time to time that, if I did have to do without her, Frank might have to do the school run occasionally. Might have to babysit. Might even change a nappy. Although even as I say it, I realise I'm being unfair, because only this morning he changed an unusually unpleasant one.

He *says* he changed *all* the nappies when his first two were babies. When I got him to agree to having our first child together, I promised to do all the nappies and take full responsibility for her care and upkeep. In so doing, I may have negotiated a rotten deal for myself. Or have I boxed Frank into an impossible corner, because in indulging him in his zeal to escape the horrible fate of househusband, I have managed to exclude him from any decision about children or money? If the answer is yes, it does not bode well for our allegedly equal partnership.

I also work harder than he does. At least this year. At least until I burn out — a fantasy that has kept me going through many bad weeks. I can tell you one thing — I don't work this hard by choice. Forget all that nonsense about self-fulfilment. That's an occasional luxury bonus. People who knew me in my lazy and morose days are always asking how do I do it. My answer is why do I have to. But here we bumble on to yet another feminist landmine. Moving quickly to avoid it, I am forced to admit that, actually, I didn't have to. My only way out is to argue that I was boomeranged into this way of life by my already set-in-psychic-granite gendered consciousness.

Although this leaves me without an excuse for my next problem: this unbelievably hostile letter from my accountant. He wrote to me about a cheque he needed a week ago. I forgot to send it. Now he's threatening to put the matter in the hands of his solicitors. How appalling. Doesn't he know how hard it is to do work, let alone up-to-date accounts, with this chaos always intruding? He assumes that we all enjoy quiet offices with full-time secretaries. How long would he last if he had to work here? Actually, don't ask. If he had to live here, he'd have it running his way in a matter of days. He is efficient by nature, just as I am inefficient by nature. And inefficient partly due to being too distractible and accommodating. Just as he is efficient because he thinks of himself first. I imagine that, in this better household, *he* would still be the one reading the paper, and *I* would still be the one shepherding children into the car.

As I do just this, I cannot fail to notice that the one child Frank says goodbye to is *his* daughter Rachel. While they linger in their embrace, my daughter Emma stamps her feet, allegedly because she can't find her clarinet. But I suspect because the embrace makes her feel unloved and excluded. Is this why I jump to her defence when Frank shouts at her? Or is it just a bit more personal and primitive? Once, when Helen was a baby and Pandora still a terrified glint in her father's eye, Frank told me that he felt closer to *his* children than he did to *our* daughter. No longer true – but the remark lives on. Am I wrong to feel jealous? Right to feel guilty? I'd say it doesn't matter so long as I protect my stepdaughter from my feelings. Which I do. Actually – overdo. Look, for example, at the gentle way I talk to Rachel as I help her into the car. When my Emma protests (jealous again?) I snap at her. Which (to borrow her favourite expression) just isn't fair. You want to know how I manage to look after so many children? Easy – I just do it badly.

So this is what it's come to. Once I assumed I knew exactly how to change the world. Now I get through the day. And the most taxing part of it all is not feeding the children or clothing the children or even finding the time and space in which to work. It's the interior monologue, which, if I transcribed it, would read like a woman's page run amok. I can't walk from one end of my kitchen to the other without querying my motives or comparing myself unfavourably with two warring tribes of ideal types. If I leave the house without clearing up the breakfast dishes, I'm a bad housekeeper. If I do clear them, I'm a pushover, because really I ought to have asked Frank. If he clears them without my asking, then I'm luckier, at least according to the latest statistics, than 97 per cent of women in this country. If I forget to thank him, I'm a shrew. If I do thank him, I'm setting up the expectation that household chores, if he does them, are favours, and not duties, and so I become my own worst enemy. And – oh yes – also a bad mother, because of the shoes I allowed to go unpolished, the playdates I forgot to make, that clarinet that went missing as a result of my bad budgeting of time and attention.

What I am describing is not, I suspect, much different from the web my parents and grandparents and great-grandparents weaved around themselves as they waited their turn in the confession box. I neither like nor trust people who never examine their consciences, or people who never hold themselves accountable for their actions, but when I look at the people in my family who are still good Catholics, I can see how docile this habit of thought has made them. I can see how convenient this docility is for everyone else. It occurs to me, therefore, that my own soul-searching has a similar effect on me and is similarly convenient. The more I fret about the political implications of my private life, the more I allow the teeming school of feminist debating points to attack my life like so many piranha fish, the less energy I have to think about the ways in which I am unequivocally exploited.

You could argue that this is as much my fault as everything else is. I would welcome this criticism with my usual open arms – but point out too that I am not alone here. That the type of maternal soul-searching I have described is so deeply ingrained in most of us that twenty-five years of feminist finger-pointing has had almost no effect on it. You could almost imagine that the anti-male finger-pointing is strident precisely because it exists to counterbalance the silent and so ever-growing suspicion that lives in every exploited female heart – that actually, it's all her fault. Litanies of sin, litanies of male brutality, are desperately boring unless you can't bear to look in the mirror without them.

I can look at other mothers and see that they are blaming themselves unnecessarily. But I can't seem to manage to do myself the same favour. What is wrong with me? Why can't I stop lacerating myself? I couldn't tell you. But it does seem clear that the questions I am asking myself are not the right ones. Even when they are the right ones, they become meaningless and dangerously double-edged in the absence of – what do you call it? – a stable theoretical framework. So much so that I find myself unable even to describe my own life. I'm very good at criticising people who describe it inaccurately, or who make assumptions without bothering to observe it. But when I try to set them straight, my own observations waver hysterically between bitter complaint and sentimentality.

You don't understand how hard it is/how much we've done against the odds! I moan until I've managed to convince them. Then I say but I have no regrets! This is my life! I wouldn't have it any other way!

I shouldn't blame myself, I know, for failing to rise to a

challenge that no one else has managed to rise to either. Families are, after all, complicated things. Put eight people around a breakfast table and already you have enough secrets and riddles to last you a lifetime. Put a woman at one end of the table and tell her to bring that family into line with feminist ideas of equality, equity, freedom and justice and what you have is a tragic farce. Even if you think – and I certainly do not – that she has the power to bring about such changes single-handed, and assume that she, unlike the rest of us, has a clear idea of the wonderful family that might result from these changes; if she tries to understand her raw material, and locate and remedy problems, using the crude analytical tools bequeathed to her by second-wave feminism, she will find them woefully lacking. The image that comes to mind is a woman trying to perform open-heart surgery on herself with a wrench and a crowbar.

I think even Marilyn would agree that we can't go on like this.

Part Two

Reflections of a Feminist Guinea-pig

3

THE ORIGINAL IDEA

On lectures, betrayals and new starts

I can imagine Marilyn sitting across from me on the banquette at Claridge's, balancing that long brown cigarette between two pensive fingers, and saying, 'I think it's important before we pursue this any further to take a breather. Sit back. Restore some sense of perspective. You sound very bitter, you know. What I mean is that you're reading a lot of personal problems into a historical impasse that really is quite straightforward. Now, of course, you're tired, and exasperated, and very angry. What woman in your place wouldn't be? But you are confusing the issue here. You can't reconcile your own emotional needs with the hard truths about patriarchy. There is one little three-letter word standing between you and the kind of life you deserve. That word is m-e-n. Feminists have been trying to make something out of motherhood from the very beginning. Generation after generation they have had the living daylights knocked out of them by you know who. And also by women who, for the best of reasons, have put their trust in the men they look up to and the men they love, and stopped resisting, only to find themselves right back where their mothers were. You talk about the tools of analysis not working. Well, the reason they don't work, dear, is that they were made by men. I hope you don't think I'm trying to diminish your achievements. I think you should be proud of what you've done, but you must also accept that you were aiming for the impossible.'

To which I imagine myself gathering the courage to say yes, but I thought we were aiming for the impossible together!

That was the beauty of it!

It was never a question of *having* it all. It was a question of challenging it all. All of us, everywhere. Including mothers. At the beginning of the second wave, even mothers could consider themselves part of the mainstream – even, for a brief window of opportunity, fashionable. In the late seventies and early eighties, when existentialism was beginning to look dated, when the wisdom of separatism was still debatable, when postmodernism was little more than a puzzling word, there was a serious, if short-lived, feminist effort to save the virtues and values of mothering, and therefore the world, from the traditional evils of motherhood.

The writer who laid the groundwork for these maternal radicals was Dorothy Dinnerstein. In *The Mermaid and the Minotaur*, which came out in 1976, she suggested that, from time immemorial, our sexual arrangements, or in other words, the 'division of responsibility, opportunity, and privileges' between men and women, had emanated from 'a core fact that has so far been universal': that women cared for infants and small children. These arrangements had underpinned and shaped our history, made us into what we were. Although they continued to provide much of 'our pleasure in living', they had never been comfortable. They had been a constant source of 'pain, fear, and hate' and friction between men and women 'as far back into time as the study of myth and ritual permits us to trace human feeling'.[1] Hence the symbols in her title:

> The treacherous mermaid, seductive and impenetrable female representative of the dark and magic underwater world from which our life comes and in which we cannot live, lures voyagers to their doom. The fearsome minotaur, gigantic and eternally infantile offspring of a mother's unnatural lust, male representative of mindless, greedy power, insatiably devours live human flesh.[2]

Put them together, she said, and they signified:

> ... our longstanding general awareness of our uneasy, ambiguous position in the animal kingdom [and] a more

REFLECTIONS OF A FEMINIST GUINEA-PIG

specific awareness: that until we grow strong enough to renounce the pernicious prevailing forms of collaboration between the sexes, both man and woman will remain semi-human, monstrous.[3]

But her aim was not to save the world by making men and women whole and happy. Her aim was to prevent the end of the world. She believed that it was our present sexual arrangements that had brought the human race to the edge of extinction. She hoped that, if she could make this clear, to feminists and radicals if to no one else, then she would be able to give these readers the vision and moral backbone they needed to work together to create new sexual arrangements, and a new, life-affirming world.

At the time of writing, she felt that both vision and backbone were lacking. People were either clinging blindly to the old arrangements, or abandoning them in disgust. Her first mission, then, was to explain why. Like so many French feminists, and even like Betty Friedan, she saw the breakdown of the gender contract as having taken place slowly, and in fits and starts, over two centuries. Unlike Betty Friedan, she did not see our present troubles as having originated in the suffocating doll's houses of the fifties suburb. The murderous jolt that gave birth to the discontents of second-wave feminism was, she said, Hiroshima. Or more specifically, 'the possibility, which exploded into public awareness at Hiroshima, that we are the last generation'. The young adults who were its shocked witnesses had, she said, 'been largely inarticulate about the ways in which this explosion – and the light it shed on the period that led up to it – determined for them the quality of the years that followed'. And it was during those years, 'steeped in what remained centrally unspoken, that the young adults of the new left – including the passionate, determined new feminists – were growing up.'[4] Their 'mute spiritual progenitors' included many prewar radicals who had slumped, postwar, into a:

... state of moral shock: that is, in the condition of anaesthesia and blurred comprehension that follows cata-strophe... They withdrew from history – more or less totally, more or less gradually, more or less blindly – into intensely personalistic, inward-turning magically thing-and-place oriented life.

By this she insisted that she did not mean 'the simple greed, the herd-minded preoccupation with material prosperity, that characterise mainstream American life'. She was speaking of the left, of:

> . . . a particular group of people, in historic despair so deep that few of us could recognise it clearly as despair, for whom a few beloved things and places came to be quasi-symbolic centres of connectedness to humanity.[5]

Doris Lessing described this way of life most accurately, she said, in *The Four-Gated City*. But it was not just a problem for the left. Hiroshima affected everybody and was the shadow of the bright routines of the Candides who peopled the fifties suburbs. Dorothy Dinnerstein used the term 'domestic mystique' in polite opposition to Betty Friedan's feminine mystique. She also suggested (rather too politely, if you ask me) that the feminine mystique may not have been a simple postwar conspiracy to get women back into the kitchen, but part of a 'central shift in sensibility'[6] after the atom bomb. The new sensibility embodied 'two streams of feeling' that remained 'largely unreconciled except in certain general principles'. The first was 'that expressive, aesthetic, humanistic values must shape the world, that eroticism must permeate history' instead of being 'encapsulated in genital sex'. The second was that 'first-hand, emotionally vivid experience, not theory-dominated policy which violates such experience, must shape social action'.[7]

This shift put 'unrecognised and unusual responsibility'[8] on women and gave a new significance to the domestic realm. They were in charge of giving life meaning again, making up for the war and the bomb and the death camps and the soul-destroying functionalism of work. She believed they did make up for it. And they were proud of their achievement.

This is very much in contrast to the Betty Friedan version

which has the fifties housewives wasting away in their isolated, sexualised boxes, although it doesn't need to contradict it. Put together the two, and you have a rather larger, rather more historical picture of the problem with no name. You have a sense that somewhere, somehow, Betty's housewives knew that the exercise was futile, that the realm on which they had turned their back was still poisoned and still all-powerful. You have an explanation as to why a small percentage of discontented housewives would break away to follow B.F.'s footsteps, while those who stayed behind would become all the more adamant, and all the more protective, of the values they lived by. And why neither contingent would want to look back at the nameless horror behind them.

The real shift, according to Dinnerstein, occurred not when the fifties children rebelled against their parents but when they dared to practise in public what their parents had preached in private. 'In the youth revolution of the sixties, the values that this silent undertaking had nurtured became suddenly and exuberantly outspoken.'[9] The new generation did not just say the words – they acted on them. Dinnerstein did not relate the chain of betrayals this brought about – the parents' fury at the breaking of the silence and the shattering of the home, the children's fury at the parents' refusal to accept that there was a direct link between their upbringing and their new project, the children's labelling of their parents' mute fear as hypocrisy, their resulting rebellion, the parents' apparently heartless and spineless retreat. Instead she was concerned about what happened to the women on the left when the men on the left started to think too much like their mothers. When the 'hearth-centred' movement became a political one, female values got appropriated by the men who put themselves in charge of it. This left the women feeling 'disinherited':

Things that women have always informally and deeply known, and been heavily relied upon to affirm on an everyday, folk-knowledge level – that personal truth, one's own intuitive grasp of what is going on, is ignored at one's own grave risk; that largescale politics are pompous and farcical; that science and logic are a limited and overrated part of our array of techniques for exploring reality; that face-to-face relations are in a basic sense the point of life; that flowers, gossip, the smell of food, the smiling of babies, embody and symbolise central human values – men now seized from their hands and made into a big and characteristically overblown deal, a newly discovered historic tool too significant for women to wield except as man's assistants.[10]

She felt that the new-left men had no choice but to do what they did, and that what they did was begin to redefine the traditional male role. In rejecting many traditional male responsibilities, they began to:

[her italics] *usurp many aspects of traditional feminine authority. At the same time, they remained understandably unwilling to relinquish traditional male privileges. This left women stripped of old forms of support, respect and protection, and of old outlets for self-assertion, but still as disparaged, subordinated and exploited as ever.*

Men had changed but their desires had not. Because of their upbringing, what they continued to value in women was 'maternal applause, menial services and body contact'.[11] Except that now they were hoping to get all this without having to turn into their workaholic fathers, into slump-shouldered breadwinners whose idea of fun was presiding over a suburban barbecue. Despite their withdrawal from the traditional responsibilities of marriage, they still found hard to accept in women all those traits that women needed to develop if they were going to make their own way in a man's world – and if they were going to help men change it.

When the women in the movement worked out what was going on, and what these developments spelled for their place in the scheme of things, they were convulsed with rage. But the feminist movement would have been revived at around this time anyway:

Women have a long tradition of trying to be part of formal history (instead of continuing to act as safety valves for everyone's suppressed loathing of the form this has taken).[12]

But the men failed to take the rage seriously. Even though they were putting themselves on the line at rallies and sit-ins, and rebelling 'at great personal sacrifice against and within the military itself', even though they expressed their new views not just politically but in 'their speech styles and clothing, in the psychedelic music and drug states, and their growth of masses of hair' – they could not understand why it was just as important to 'start outgrowing the collaboration between the sexes that . . . made the development of this poisoned realm possible' and let women change too. This was what caused the 'rift' between the sexes:

It insulted and disinherited, in personally intolerable ways, the women who could have worked with them as peers. [And made the] old heterosexual arrangement . . . become in an intimate way – a way that has to do with a person's sense of history, but that throws the person personally off-balance, too, in a way that hurts the felt inner core of individuality – unworkable.

At the same time, both men and women felt the pressure of 'the historical impasse' of which the rift was but a part:

That the world-making enterprise, traditionally a male responsibility, is now in unprecedented trouble is a fact that hits men harder . . . what hits women harder . . . is the way this unprecedented trouble undermines our private modes of connectedness to past and future. [Their role as] living link between grandparents and grandchildren, the care work they do at births, weddings and funerals to nurture the intimate ties that link the old and the young, the unborn and the dead, is disrupted.

At the same time, they could depend less on the guidance of their own parents, as they were 'forced to feel out ways of living in a world that their elders cannot begin to conceive of'. This hit them hard as it 'undermined the female sense of human importance that has till now derived from the task of maintaining the intimate bridge between the generations, a bridge on which formal worldmaking, and humanness itself, ultimately rests'. The domestic realm had become discredited. This was how to account for:

> ... The virulent reckless, reactive quality of the new feminist rhetoric against the biological family, against permanent personal commitments of adults to children ... indeed against bodily childbearing itself ... Shorn of its humanising significance, the sheer biological continuity of the species becomes an unacceptable burden; the lifebearing, lactating mammalian heritage becomes monstrous. Some women come to feel like jumping out of their very bodies, out of their very inconvenient skins.

This was understandable:

> Cut off from her family, cut off from her possible children, cut out of history itself because her special, traditional, compartmentalised contribution to the historical process is pre-empted by man, who sees that this contribution to the historical process is overdue for integration but is not ready to work with her as a simple equal ... how can a woman feel?[13]

Betrayed. Not for the first time, but — she had convinced herself — possibly for the last. As the old male–female collaboration crumbled, so too were crumbling all the social and political arrangements that depended on it. That was why it was important, Dinnerstein felt, to look forward as well as backwards. Why it was so important to understand why we came to this:

> My effort here is to see what it is that we're so sad about: on the one hand what there is in the dying old arrangement that we will all have to outgrow or die ourselves and on the other hand what there is in it that we all legitimately need, that we

cannot and should not try to do without and that we must therefore find other ways of getting.[14]

I have quoted Dinnerstein at length not because I accept her every word as gospel but because it puts the story of my life into a context I can recognise, and more particularly describes the mood of the time, and the way people then thought about the future, and therefore about children. I am a product of a string of odd, ill-matched and atypical historical accidents – born in New Jersey to Irish-American parents, I grew up in Istanbul, went back to the US for university only to return to Europe within days of graduation – but even so the account she describes was going on in all those places and I was a witness to it. My father was in the war. When my father met my mother, they turned their back on the war. They lived in fifties suburbs. When I was small, my father worked as a physicist in a military project. When it was almost entirely depopulated of physicists during the McCarthy era, he moved on to Project Matterhorn at Princeton – to be closer to his hero, Einstein. But Einstein died the day we moved there.

My mother didn't mind. Her life took off. It was the only time, she told me later, that she was part of a society of women, and these were women with an amazing array of interests and activities. She now says she wishes she had been twins so that she could have lived out her years in Princeton twice over.

My father was too busy to enjoy it. He was still doing his degree at the time at New York University. His professors were mainly Jewish refugees from Germany. Some had been involved in the atom bomb. When he got a job teaching in Istanbul, the idea was to get away from all that, to make a new and better life, but just for our family, and eventually for our small, very unconventional expatriate paradise. Never more than that. We lived in a refuge, but even the refuge was not safe. When the Soviet Union sent missiles to Cuba, the ships went right in front of our house. We were half a world away from Kennedy when he was assassinated, half a world away from civil rights and the war against the war in Vietnam. But our community was still torn apart by these things. The only difference was that the newspapers came two days late – and that these newspapers were often our only sources.

They did not report the early days of the women's liberation movement in a way that made them real to me. I had, literally, missed the sixties. I was not prepared for the war I walked into when I went back to attend Radcliffe in 1970. I could not reconcile the ideals that everyone, including me, professed with the horrible things people were doing to each other. Most particularly, I was disturbed about a woman I babysat for. I walked into her family at exactly the same time that she undertook to in her words, liberate herself. In fact, I was the person who made it possible. I watched the family fall apart in front of my eyes. I could not understand how ideals that were mine as much as they were hers could lead to such disaster. I did not understand the hatred she suddenly had for her husband. I could not understand how she could justify entertaining her lover in front of her children while her husband slept on the couch in the study. I could not live with the ever-growing mental barriers she put between herself and her children, and consequently, because by then I was one of her children, me.

The last straw for me was the day her youngest let himself out of the house to drink from a container of petrol that had been left on the porch. I caught him doing it, spent the rest of the afternoon doing what the doctors said to counteract the poison. I told his mother what had happened as soon as she walked through the door that evening. Hmm, she said. Sounds like you did the right thing. With that she put down her handbag and picked up the telephone. I couldn't understand how a mother who was human could do that. I could not imagine the betrayal that had turned her into a monster, turned everyone into monsters. By the time I did, I had been betrayed in as many ways by as many hypocrites as everyone else.

Except for the man I married: his life contained its own history of betrayals. His father, a Protestant minister and civil rights leader, had been murdered at the age of forty-two in 1966, when Paul was nineteen and in his second year at Columbia. (The murder remains unsolved to this day.) Paul had decided he wanted to be a writer when he was still a teenager, and by the time he was in college, had begun publishing short stories and articles in places like the *Paris Review* and *Village Voice*. His first book came out the same year he graduated. Shortly thereafter, he and his girlfriend got married. The marriage only lasted a year. Paul moved to Europe, where he wrote a book about his father. I met him in Greece just a few weeks after this book was published, in 1973, the summer before my last year at Radcliffe. It was also a few days before my twenty-first birthday. He gave me a copy to read. I fell in love with him while reading it. The book's last lines were, 'Father, I cannot understand your death.'

I had always wanted, but rarely dared, to write. He gave me the courage to try. We were able to go to Europe within days of my graduation because he had just won a grant to write a novel about freedom. We took two Olivetti typewriters. Mine was a dull blue-green Lettera, his a bright-red Valentine. When we got to Spain, he set his up in the bedroom, and I set mine up in the sitting room. We worked identical hours, made money doing the same kind of temporary jobs, as we moved on first to Istanbul, then to London, Lesbos, New York, Chicago, and London again. My first novel never got published. We decided to have a child at about the same time I started work on the second one. To pay for it, Paul sold an idea for a thriller about Franklin Roosevelt. We finished the books in the same week. I found out I was pregnant on the same day I found out I had sold my novel.

The novel was about children, sexual politics, and betrayal. It ends with the heroine getting kicked rather quickly and summarily out of the house where she has been working as a mother's helper. As she walks through the snow in unsuitable sandals, she tries to walk in other people's footsteps as often as possible. And that was my idea, our idea of having a baby. The idea of having a baby illustrated the central question. Or rather, it was impossible to conceive of a baby without returning again and again to the tangled web of central questions: How to carry on living, and trusting in life, if you've been betrayed? How to believe in anything if you can't believe in God, if you can't trust anything or anyone? How to keep faith in the future if the past and the present are so corrupt? How to know when it's right to walk in other people's footsteps, when it's right to strike out on your own? How to know what to pass on to your children, and what to throw out the window so that it never hurts them?

I was not worried about my own working future because I knew that childcare was not going to be a problem: Paul and I were going to bring up our much-desired child the same way we did everything, which was together. It went without saying that the child would enjoy immeasurable benefits from having two primary parents, and that the child with two primary parents was the child who would never suffer from betrayal, or indeed any civilized neurosis or discontent. That this child would go on to be an architect of the new dawn. These were not just products of our naive and fevered imaginations. These were the ideas that people took seriously in those days. They were validated by Dorothy Dinnerstein, who saw the only hope for the future in the image of a man and a woman rocking the cradle together. And in 1978, this same image was translated into theory by Nancy Chodorow, who saw a new world order as emerging from shared parenting. In this glorious future where neither girls nor boys were ever too autonomous nor too dependent, masculinity would no longer be linked to the 'denial of dependence and devaluation of women'. Children would no longer think of their mothers as omnipotent or women as self-sacrificing. Men would no longer need to 'guard their masculinity and their control of social and cultural spheres which treat and define women as secondary and powerless'. Instead, they would 'help women to develop the autonomy which too much embeddedness in relationship has often taken from them'.

Equal parenting would give all children more freedom to develop their own identities, she insists in her starry-eyed conclusion. It would:

> . . . leave people of both genders with the positive capacities each has, but without the destructive extremes these currently tend toward. Anyone who has a good primary relationship has the foundation for nurturance and love, and women would retain these even as men would gain them . . . People's sexual choices might become more flexible, less desperate.

I would like to think we could simply initiate these transformations on a society-wide scale.[15]

This was unlikely in the short term, so it was all the more important for individual parents to act on her ideas. It was up to them to do their bit to combat gender inequality.

Yes, that was how people thought in these days. If you wanted to save the world, if you wanted to repair the damage, if you wanted to prove that feminism did not lead inexorably to a child with a container of petrol, if you wanted some good to come out of evil, if you wanted to make a contribution to the cause, however vague that cause might have become by the late seventies – if you wanted to give that cause a new lease on life, you had a baby.

A parent of some experience might have been able to read and even appreciate these idealistic directives while also imagining the practical difficulties they might lead to. She might also have picked up on the mistrust of traditional mothering that their authors continued to exude, almost in spite of themselves, and wondered what this horror was that they all seemed so keen never to name or view directly. I did not see any of these problems, and when older, wiser people brought them up I dismissed them as nitpickers.

All I saw was the invitation. And just as I did not see where it might lead, neither did I see how it did not sit happily with the other invitation that went out at about the same time. This one was from the radicals of body politics, who, for a brief period during the late seventies, went maternal to a degree people would now call sentimental.

The body vs. the institution of motherhood

Like Betty, and Marilyn, and so many of their lesser-known followers, Adrienne Rich began adult life as a housebound mother. She remembers it as a time when she was constantly being pulled in two directions. There was the longing to escape from the tedium, and from the circular time-keeping of domesticity, into the straight-arrow world of thought and action. Because that world was forbidden, she was, she wrote in her diary of the time, 'weak sometimes from held-in rage'. Maternal bonds turned into chains:

> There are times when I feel only death will free us from one another, when I envy the barren woman who has the luxury of her regrets but lives a life of privacy and freedom . . .[16]
>
> And yet other times, I am melted with the sense of their helpless, charming and quite irresistible beauty – their ability to go on loving and trusting – their staunchness and decency and unselfconsciousness. *I love them*. But it's in the enormity and inevitability of this that the sufferings lie.[17]

The 'concentration camp' she was living in at the time was Cambridge, Massachusetts – more comfortable, you might have thought, than most, at least for the woman seeking intellectual stimulation. Her memories recorded in *Of Woman Born* indicate otherwise:

> I was struggling to bring my life into focus. I had never really given up on poetry, nor on gaining some control over my existence. The life of a Cambridge tenement backyard, swimming with children, the repetitious cycles of laundry, the night wakings, the interrupted moments of peace or of engagement with ideas, the ludicrous dinner parties at which young wives, some with advanced degrees, all seriously and intelligently dedicated to their children's welfare and their husbands' careers, attempted to reproduce the amenities of Brahmin Boston, amid French recipes and the pretence of effortlessness – above all, the ultimate lack of seriousness with which women were regarded in that world – all of this defied analysis at that time, but I *knew* I had to remake my own life.[18]

One summer, when her husband ('a sensitive, affectionate man' who was often willing to 'help'[19]) had to be away for several weeks, she and her three sons went to stay in a house in Vermont. Here, for the first time, they were able to escape from the hated treadmill. They fell into a 'delicious and sinful rhythm'. They ate outdoors, 'lived half-naked', stayed up late at night, looking at bats and stars and fireflies:

> . . . like castaways on some island of mothers and children . . . I remember thinking: This is what living with children could be – without school hours, fixed routines, naps, the conflict of being both mother and wife with no room for being, simply, myself.

Coming home late one night from a drive-in movie, 'through the foxfire and stillness of a winding Vermont road', with three sleeping children in the back of a car, she thought triumphantly of all the rules they had broken:

> We were conspirators, outlaws from the institution of motherhood; I felt enormously in charge of my life. Of course, the institution closed down on us again and my own mistrust of myself as a 'good mother' returned, along with my resentment of the archetype. But I knew even then that I did not want my sons to act for me in the world, any more than I wished for them to kill or die for their country. I wanted to act, to live, in myself and to love them for their separate selves.[20]

Money was not an issue for her – in the time-honoured tradition of people who can take material comforts for granted – what she cared about was *fulfilment. Self-expression. Authentic experience. The truth.* The way forward, she eventually decided, was to take back the power stolen from us in the name of the Institution of Motherhood.[21]

Her mother was a classic victim of this theft. She had given up her career as pianist the better to serve her transcendentalist doctor father. He had his own ideas about childrearing:

> I believe that my mother . . . at first genuinely and enthusiastically embraced the experiment, and only later found that in carrying out my father's intense, perfectionist programme, she was in conflict with her deep instincts as a mother . . .

she must have found that while ideas might be unfolded by her husband, their daily, hourly practice was going to be up to her . . .

Moreover, her husband's views kept her constantly wondering if she were doing a good job:

Under the institution of motherhood, the mother is the first to blame if theory proves unworkable in practice, or if anything whatsover goes wrong.'[22]

Guilt seems to have made her into a puppet. 'For years, I felt my mother had chosen my father over me, had sacrificed me to his needs and theories.' Compassion, and with it, the more important acceptance of her desperate need for her mother, took years to attain:

Many of us were mothered in ways we cannot yet even perceive; we only know that our mothers were in some incalculable way on our side. But if a mother had deserted us . . . whatever our rational forgiveness, whatever the individual mother's love or strength, the child in us, the small female who grew up in a male-controlled world, still feels, at moments, wildly unmothered. When we can confront and unravel this paradox, this contradiction, face to the utmost in ourselves the groping passion of that little girl lost, we can begin to transmute it, and the blind anger and bitterness that have repetitiously erupted among women trying to build a movement together can be alchemised. Before sisterhood, there was the knowledge – transitory, fragmented, perhaps, but original and crucial – of mother-and-daughterhood.[23]

'This cathexis between mother and daughter – essential, distorted, misused – is the great unwritten story,' she gushes.[24]

Probably there is nothing in human nature more resonant with charges than the flow of energy between two biologically alike bodies, one of which has lain in amniotic bliss inside the other, one of which has laboured to give birth to the other.

The materials are here for the deepest mutuality and the most painful estrangement.[25]

What concerns her most here is what to make of the history of estrangement. How to overcome the betrayals that complicate the history of the institution of motherhood, and that therefore make it so hard to overturn. How to reaffirm the connection between the daughter and the colluding mother. How to appreciate her mother, and all mothers, for what they did in spite of being forced into mental slavery. How to identify, and then treasure the maternal gifts that somehow managed to get past the internal and external patriarchal censors.

'It is hard for me to write about my own mother,' she admits. (And what daughter could say differently?) 'I know the deep reservoirs of anger toward her still exist . . .'[26]

And I know there must be deep reservoirs of anger in her, every mother has known overwhelming unacceptable anger at her children. When I think of the conditions under which my mother became a mother, the impossible expectations, my father's distaste for pregnant women, his hatred of all that he could not control, my anger at her dissolves into grief and anger *for* her, and then dissolves back into anger at her: the ancient, unpurged anger of the child.[27]

It is hard for her to write about her own mother, but she gets to the truth of what she calls the double vision in a way that must make every daughter tremble. She does not go quite as far with her unwitting spiritual mother, Simone de Beauvoir. Although she pays tribute to this woman as one of many childless feminists, who 'precisely because they were not bound to the cycle of hourly existence with children, because they could reflect, observe, write . . . have given us some of the few available strong insights into the experience of women in general' and without whom 'we would all today be suffering from spiritual malnutrition',[28] she is too polite (and too afraid?) to say that her idea of the future was born of her decision to turn the Simone de Beauvoir doctrine inside out.

When we get to this point of the story, I always imagine

WHAT ABOUT US?

Adrienne and Simone sitting together in Aux Deux Magots. Simone is drinking Pernod and exhaling Gauloises through her nostrils; Adrienne, who can't stand inconsiderate smokers, is nonetheless shifting her chair and her stance so as to keep her anxious smile from turning into a cough. She listens with filial devotion as Simone pontificates, struggling to extract the pearls of protofeminism while shuddering like a Geiger counter whenever Simone unthinkingly colludes with her oppressors. This is never more so than when Simone is on the subject of pregnancy, which she describes as a sort of subdermal Greek tragedy:

It is, she claims, 'above all a drama that is acted out within the woman herself'. The baby is a sort of fatal flaw:

> She feels it as at once an enrichment and an injury; she is possessed *of* it, and she is possessed by it; it represents the future and, carrying it, she feels herself vast as the world but this very opulence annihilates her, she feels that she herself is no longer anything. A new life is going to manifest itself and justify its own separate existence, she is proud of it; but she also feels herself tossed and driven, the plaything of obscure forces.[29]

Lurching grandly now into the language of existentialism – to please whom? – Simone now says:

> It is especially noteworthy that the pregnant woman feels the immanence of her own body at just the time when it is in transcendence: it turns in upon itself in nausea and discomfort; it has ceased to exist for itself and thereupon becomes more sizeable than ever before.

Tying herself up in some rather large theoretical knots now, but cleverly projecting them into the hypothetical mother who is the object of her contempt, she continues:

> The transcendence of the artisan or the man of action contains the element of subjectivity; but in the mother-to-be the antithesis of subject and object ceases to exist; she and

the children with whom she is swollen make up together an equivocal pair overwhelmed by life. Ensnared by nature, the pregnant woman is plant and animal, a stockpile of colloids, an incubator, an egg: she scares children proud of their young, straight bodies and makes young people titter contemptuously because she is a human being, a conscious and free individual, who has become life's passive instrument.[30]

Pausing now to take the last Gauloise from the pack, she intones:

Creative acts originating in liberty establish the object as value and give it the quality of the essential; whereas the child in the maternal body is not thus justified; it is still only a gratuitous cellular growth, a brute fact of nature as contingent on circumstance as death and corresponding philosophically with it.[31]

Brandishing her cigarette, flashing her best bad-fairy smile, she reminds her wincing acolyte how ominously significant it is that woman requires help in performing the function assigned to her by nature: 'At just the time when woman attains the realisation of her feminine destiny, she is still dependent.'[32]

Just as she forgave her mother by emphasising the power her father held over her, Adrienne Rich forgives Simone (without ever daring to mention her by name) by deflecting blame to the men who formed her mind:

The ancient, continuing envy, awe and dread of the male for the female capacity to create life has repeatedly taken the form of hatred for every other female aspect of creativity ... No wonder that many intellectual and creative women have insisted that they were 'human beings' first and women only incidentally.[33]

As wrong as she might have been about some things, Adrienne says, Simone was right about others: 'It was as Mother that woman was fearsome,' she quotes Simone as saying, 'it is in maternity that she must be transfigured and enslaved.'[34] And if maternity has been 'domesticated' throughout history, if the source of this power, the womb, 'has been historically turned against us and itself made into a source of powerlessness',[35] the obvious solution is to regain control of it.

The idea of the reclaimed and politically reconstituted body was a familiar one when *Of Woman Born* came out in 1976. Norman O. Brown had floated the idea in the sixties, and so had Herbert Marcuse. It informed the Institute of Consciousness that the two men founded at Santa Cruz. You could say it was the founding idea of the human potential movement. But Adrienne Rich is dismissive of its male creators. They were too vague, she claims. They enthused about the feminine principle, but like her own father, they cared little about the practical application beyond their concern that someone else oversaw the minutiae. Her own recommendations were not for a world reordered according to a feminine principle so much as a world turned upside-down, and so restored to its proper order, by feminine thinking. The first step was to understand the degree to which the physical was political: 'The woman's body is the terrain on which patriarchy is erected.'[36] The next step was to unlearn everything we have ever learned about our bodies:

> Patriarchal thought has limited female biology to its own narrow specifications. The feminist vision has recoiled from female biology for these reasons; it will, I believe, come to view our physicality as a resource rather than as a destiny.

Echoing the authors of *Our Bodies, Ourselves*, which was, in those days, every feminist coed's bible, and which incidentally, did not originally include a chapter on fertility, she says:

> In order to live a fully human life we require not only *control* of our bodies (though control is a prerequisite); we must touch the unity and resonance of our physicality, our bond with the natural order, the corporeal ground of our intelligence.[37]

Having reclaimed the original site of oppression, we then face the daunting task of understanding it. But in arguing:

... that we have by no means yet explored or understood our biological grounding, the miracle and paradox of the female body and its spiritual and political meanings, I am really asking whether women cannot begin at last, to *think through the body*, to connect what has been so cruelly disorganised – our great mental capacities, hardly used; our genius for close observation, our complicated, pain-enduring, multi-pleasured physicality.[38]

'Physical motherhood is merely one dimension of our being,' she reminds us. But to reject the body just because it can turn you into a mother is a terrible mistake. 'The fear and hatred of our bodies has often crippled our brains,' she says. In another side allusion to Simone, she adds:

Some of the most brilliant women of our time are still trying to think from somewhere outside their female bodies – hence they are still merely reproducing old forms of intellection.[39]

This was what was going to have to stop if we were to save feminism from a spiritual miscarriage, and get it to focus on its true task, the transformation of the world. How this battle would or should be waged, what part men would play in this drama, what would happen to them afterwards – all these matters she left typically vague so as better to inspire a more diverse audience. Despite that fact that she herself is a lesbian, and despite the fact that, if you followed her advice to the letter, you would have to become at least a political lesbian, there is never a sense that she is preaching solely to the converted. Here is her grand and curiously militaristic send-off:

The repossession by women of our bodies will bring far more essential change to human society than the seizing of the means of production by workers. The female body has been both territory and machine, virgin wilderness to be exploited and assembly line turning out life. *We need to imagine a world in which every woman is the presiding genius of her own body.* [My italics] In such a world women will truly create new life, bringing forth not only children (if and as we choose) but the visions, and the thinking, necessary to sustain, console and alter human existence – a new relationship to the universe. Sexuality, politics, intelligence, power, motherhood, work, community, intimacy, will develop new meanings; thinking itself will be transformed.

This is where we have to begin.[40]

Despite my congenital impatience with such high-minded lectures, these were, nonetheless, the tangled ideas I took with me into pregnancy.

4

THE ONE, THE OTHER, AND THE BABY

A few short confessions

I

Thick blue floor-length curtains, closed. Sticking out from underneath them, a yellowing rolled-up newspaper that a previous tenant must have used as a draught-excluder. Inside, taking up most of the floor, two unequal mattresses trying to share a box-spring that once belonged to a double bed. And there, propped up on the pillows on the side next to the lamp table, surrounded by paperback pregnancy manuals, I can see my innocent, and oh so infuriating former self.

The things I wish I could tell her! Get up. Open the curtains. Let in the sun! Stop wallowing. Put away those stupid books. If you want to use this time to get prepared, forget the experts. Find a *real* baby. And while you're at it, stop fixating on childbirth! For God's sake, you'd think you were going for a doctorate in labour-management! When are you going to get it through your thick skull that no one's going to give you a diploma for your efforts, that the birth is not the end but the beginning?

I wish I could tell her those things, but at the same time I can remember the other view: the dark, threatening, uncontrollable room, the curtains that part at the top to let in a sliver of sunlight so sharp it seems to slice my eyes, the makeshift draught-excluder that I would like to remove but can't because it is self-evident that if I were up to the challenge I would have done so already. And there, too large now to avoid, serving as a not entirely satisfactory bookrest, my former abdomen.

My body, but not myself. No longer answerable to my brain, it has a will of its own. Although I cannot control it, it can control me. Or rather, it can punish me, without bothering to give advance warning, whenever I do anything it doesn't want. If I walk too far, it makes me breathless. If I eat anything that contains an onion, it keeps me up all night and then refuses to get out of bed until the following afternoon. And if I try to rebel against these harsh measures, it doesn't think twice about taking punitive action against its other hostage, my unborn child.

How the hell are you supposed to *think through your body* if you don't know the first thing about it? If the history of your relationship with your body is a gothic horror story? If your body has never once done as you asked, never even listened to you? I'm sure Adrienne Rich would object to these questions, and point out that what she meant was that we needed to learn to respect and like our bodies, that to think through your body was to think holistically. But you only have to look at her language to see that she suffers from the same Cartesian split as I do. The mind is one thing, the body another. In an ideal world, the former controls the latter: *Every woman is the presiding genius over her body.*

To which I say: No pregnant woman can be the presiding genius over her body. This is not just a wrong metaphor, it is a metaphor that makes it even harder for a pregnant woman to accept, respect her body, and even more important, accept, respect the facts of life. The central thing to remember about pregnancy is that, while you can influence the outcome, you can never fix it. The forces of fertility, like the rules of mortality, are larger than will-power. There are unpalatable truths that humans have to learn to accept if they are not going to be perpetually in thrall to them. This is one of them.

Another is that the body has limits. This is a basic fact that gets lost if, like Adrienne Rich, you have decided that the body is the terrain on which patriarchy is, no pun intended, erected. If you believe that your personal and political future depend on the outcome of your struggle to repossess your body, if you are immersed in a culture that has convinced you that you are a citadel under siege, a citadel that is sure to fall if it is so foolish to admit even one of the savage Saracen sperms fighting to enter it – then it is hard to accept, if and when you do decide to have children, that getting pregnant isn't always as easy as falling to the infidel.

I mean, think about it. Here you are, A-plus student, *mens sana in corpore sano*. You've made a rational decision to become pregnant. You've thrown away the pill or the dia-phragm or whatever amulet you've been using to ward off that powerful demon called Biological Destiny. How are you going to feel if your body does what my body did for a year and a half, or rather, didn't? How confident are you going to be about using this body in future as a power-base? Infertility and subfertility are hard enough to bear if you're travelling with the horse before the cart. But if the body that has failed you is a body you've been intending to use for political purposes, it's doubly shaming.

And what happens if and when you do conceive? How can you bring yourself to trust this treacherous political wild-card to bring your precious baby to term? And what are you to make of the fact that your body, your metaphor, is daily changing shape? How are you to accept that the nature and pace of this change in shape is neither in reference nor deference to the head-of-household brain? How much help can you expect to give your sisters in struggle if you can't even keep your own site of oppression in working order? In this context, even late-afternoon fatigue becomes a leadership problem, a moral failure, and a gushing fountain of guilt. Even the gentlest reminder that the future does not promise unlimited freedom becomes the threat of a life-sentence. And this body you so desperately wanted as your best friend and most important political ally becomes your jailer.

It is no accident, it has just occurred to me, that I devoted the better part of my first pregnancy to translating the memoirs of a Turkish woman about her years in a political prison.

Guards. Threats. Body searches. Endless, meaningless days in bed. Here was a story that had far more emotional resonance for me than my peppy pregnancy books, my feminist reclaimings of the cultural meanings of maternity. These were all about resilience and perseverance and control and connection. Being in touch with your body. Responding to the first signs of new life. Being at one with the universe. Celebrating the miracle that is nature. All things I would have liked to have been doing during my long, dull and lonely maiden-voyage to term. But I couldn't, because I could not bring myself to believe that a personal and political failure such as myself could possibly be capable of creating a life.

And what was all this crap I kept reading about creativity? What the hell did these writers mean? Creativity had always meant hard work to me. It meant pushing your mind and your body to its limits. Now suddenly creativity meant doing nothing, while pushing your mind and body to their limits meant harming the baby. I lived in terror of harming the baby, and therefore in terror of acting in character. This turned me into just the sort of easily led automaton that my mother was supposed to have been. Too terrified to relax, too mistrustful of nature just to sit back and let it take its course, I policed my body, my mind – and edited out all thoughts that could be harmful to my baby, my babyish understanding of body politics. This is nowhere so clear as in that diary. It is a pathetic document that records without insight every bout of nausea, every faint spell, every ounce gained and egg half-heartedly eaten. I refused to admit I was upset about my body changing shape. Because, no, honestly, it was fine – really! Honestly, that temper tantrum was just an aberration. That crying jag must have been hormones. Please believe me when I tell you that everything else, everything else that wasn't my fault, that is, was wonderful, delightful, delicious!

> Today I am going to take a day off my eggs [I begin one entry]. I'm just not used to eating so many. Maybe I'll make a rule of skipping eggs on Saturday. That will be something to look forward to. Today I am going to have some Hero pea soup. I have already had my yoghurt and two teas and the banana which helps to prevent nausea. I don't like bananas so much as to feel a craving for them, but I certainly like them more than I used to. Just as I dislike coffee and peanut butter and anything with garlic in it, and very much enjoy frozen Bertorelli lemons and oranges and all variations of fresh fruit.

How old does this person sound to you? Twelve? Eleven? Maybe even younger? I was twenty-five years old. A world traveller, with an impressive degree and six languages. I had already written two novels, not to mention the Complete Guide to Greece. I had hundreds of amazingly amusing friends. I could shine at any dinner party with my eyes closed. I had a well-developed, and tragically cynical view of the world. I had just spent a year working in the Death Penalty Department at Amnesty International. I had an instant, and usually a very sharp, opinion on just about anything. Now here I was, as drained of ideas as I was of energy, keeping watch over my wayward and indecipherable body, keeping my dangerous brain in a strait-jacket, and appeasing the monster with daily offerings of bananas and Bertorelli lemons.

It is amazing how much different you feel when you're pregnant [the same entry continues]. And to think that so many of these emotional changes are due to hormone changes! It makes you realise what an important role hormones and chemicals play in your life. Before I was pregnant I felt very much as if my life was controlled by my mind. I was [note the tense] a cerebral person – a brain aided and sometimes hindered by the body attached to it. Perhaps not so extreme as that . . .

And here I omit an excruciatingly embarrassing list of the things I still claimed to enjoy.

. . . but still, mind came first. During the first weeks I got upset when I lost my drive to work and I was too ill to do all the things I had done before, but Paul said I should relax and rest if my body told me to rest and enjoy all the changes that were occurring and not to worry, he would take care of me. And so slowly I relaxed my expectations of what I should accomplish in a day. I stopped worrying about food and housework and chores and duties and getting up late. I now sometimes can sit back and feel very much of an animal. An animal in the good sense, in the sense of being able to sit back and feel an affinity with plants and bobcats (I saw them on television recently) and horses and dogs and goats. A very pleasant feeling to feel you can sit back and let nature take its course.

Don't worry. It doesn't last. Pantheism never does:

But on the other hand, I'm *very* mad at Paul, perhaps because he is doing just that. He drank too much again last night, and so today he has a hangover – surprise surprise – and every time I open the door to see how he's doing he complains about the white light. It is about two-thirty and he's sprawled out in bed with no intention of getting up. Now that I don't drink or smoke it seems he spends all his time drinking and smoking and gratifying his oral needs. And most of the time I put up with it with uncharacteristic silence. Perhaps it is because silence is so unnatural to me that I blow up so much when I finally can't take it any more. If only he could see what he looks like lying in bed there. I'm so mad at him I feel like crying. It is a very gloomy day and there are some idiots outside fooling around with the scaffolding. I don't think he'll even have time to do the shopping. Well, if he doesn't that's too bad because I'm not going to do it. I think I'll go to the movies by myself. I can't stand it in here.

The next entry begins: 'Well, I guess I can only sit back and let nature take its course when I'm in a good mood.'

II

Encouraged by my favourite authors, I escaped the prison that was my body by imagining the day of its liberation.

Here, finally, was a battle that promised to live up to the metaphor. Who was going to control the birth? In the good old days, I knew from countless feminist tracts and articles, this had been the domain of women. But for generations now, power had belonged to men, men, at least, in their capacity as doctors. During the fifties, they had gone too far, and all in the name of pain-management. Huh! What a joke! How did our mothers ever fall for it? They couldn't help it, presumably, on account of having been brainwashed. They had been brought up to think that the only person who knew better than Daddy was the doctor. What must it have been like for them to come out of a general anaesthetic and have to take someone else's word for it that they had given birth? How could you ever expect to bond with a baby if she wasn't in your arms when they cut the umbilical cord? If a man, and a strange man at that, had already appropriated her?

It was a question I preferred to keep rhetorical. I did not know how to go about asking my mother if she had had a hard time bonding with me. Clearly, she had managed in the end – you could argue even that she had managed too well. To know exactly what price she had paid would be to add to my already staggering list of debts. The only way to pay her back was to fight for self-determination in her honour.

And so the image crystallised: my mother, the political pawn, the innocent and unwitting site of oppression, draped like a ghost on a hospital bed, lost in a drugged dream while a team of self-made sun kings appropriated the means of reproduction. Worse than rape, and all for me! Never again, I vowed. I joined the growing chorus. From now on we wanted to be conscious, and central, and in control at this all-important moment. The woman in our braver, new ideal was upright unless she herself decided to fall back on her pillows. The person holding her hand and helping her with her breathing was not a sun king but a trusted friend, relative or partner. The room was either in the home or made warm and familiar with personal effects. Sitting unobtrusively in the corner was a supportive midwife. The air resonated with her promise not to call in a doctor or a machine unless absolutely necessary. Everything was as natural as could be. And what could be wrong with that?

If you're looking into the bubble, instead of wafting along inside it, the problems are self-evident. First of all, it is not a natural vision, but a vision in which people are able to use technology wisely, and therefore sparingly. It is also a vision that depends on consensus and co-operation. Things will only go right if the supportive midwife can count on a supportive medical service, if the woman is willing to go along with her judgement *vis-à-vis* backup and machines, and if the helpful partner agrees to be the least important person in the room – this is particularly important if he also happens to be the father. Things will go very wrong unless all these voluntary associations go like clockwork, or even better than that, *organically*. That means careful training, and intense sensitivity, and minute planning for all contingencies, all of which imply some degree of willingness to obey others if necessary. All this creates difficulties for the woman whose training has implied that birth provides a chance for creative expression, especially if she believes that it is only through creative expression that she will take back control of her body, and, oh yes, I almost forgot, forge her destiny. And in so doing, make her contribution to the war on patriarchy. And last but not least, loop back in time as well as forward to reaffirm her links with the generation upon generation of silenced matriarchs.

All this and produce a baby, too! You could almost forget, couldn't you, that the ceremony had a practical purpose. The feminist interest in questions of birth is primarily focused on the mother, and I suppose I should appreciate this for the rare occasion it is. But despite all the efforts to put her back in charge and make the experience as rich as possible, the feminist theoretical emphasis is on the larger issues, on the extent to which this woman can help in the battle for ascendancy. It's the new, improved Eleusinian Mysteries struggling to take back the night from the Cult of Dionysus. It's not just a physical birth they're after, it's a spiritual rebirth. And a cultural renaissance. In this inspiring picture, the baby is almost a pretext. A well-protected and carefully handled pretext, to be sure. But until the last act, hardly even a player. Except in the mother's head – and there's the problem.

There is a story by Mark Helprin in which a man who has just lost his family takes it upon himself to climb a mountain. But he's not in shape and he's out of practice. So what he does is set himself up in a room at the foot of the mountain with a lot of exercise equipment and prepare himself for the arduous ordeal. A few days before he is due to start the climb, he has a dream in which he begins the ascent. Over the next few nights, he dreams himself to the summit. Inspired and satisfied by this imagined view from the top, he gets up the next morning, packs his things, and heads home.

That is more or less how I approached the birth. Or rather, how I prepared to approach it. I read and reread every description I could lay my hands on. I watched every relevant programme, was tempted, when the time came to attend birth class, to go with pen and paper and take notes.

My obsession did not go unchallenged. All was not well with the man who had promised to play head of household while I went back to school. Or was it the nursery? The cot? Looking back now, it almost seems as if I was heading towards the womb. I can see now that he tried to help me: 'By the time I got back I was very tired,' I complain petulantly after describing absolutely everything I did, urine samples included, during my first visit to the hospital clinic:

I was still mad at Paul for getting mad at me because he couldn't find the oven gloves when he made my eggs, but he was very nice, and we talked about the clinic, and I had a cry about having no energy, and I had a cup of tea and two bananas, and then Paul put me to bed for a rest. For half an hour, I read the five pregnancy books Paul bought me last week, for some reason zeroing in on the chapters about ectopic pregnancies and other grotesque things like blighted ova (I kept visualising potatoes) and some failure of the ovum to differentiate, so that the whole uterus fills with a mass that looks like a thick bunch of grapes.

The next entry records the events leading up to a threatened miscarriage. I 'wore myself out dangerously' by going to the airport to collect my sister, and then by enduring:

. . . a pleasant evening – drinks at home (not me!) and dinner at the Israeli restaurant (which I found difficult to digest) and I was badly situated for cigar and cigarette smoke (three of each on either side of me). When we got home I collapsed. Paul was smashed but very kind. The next morning when I woke up there was blood in my urine.

I went straight back to bed, and over the next two hours lying in the dark trying to get back to sleep I began slowly to panic. Finally I turned on the light and read all the relevant passages in my pregnancy books and they all said to call the doctor immediately. Paul freaked out here, too. He started screaming that I needed rest, not books, and pulled the book out of my hand and threw it on the floor. Finally he calmed down and brought in the phone book and eventually got hold of a Dr Dobbs.

I report that he remained kind throughout the next thirty-six hours. But then:

On Sunday night he made roast beef and roast potatoes and a delicious salad. The meal started out badly because the meat wouldn't cut right and so as is his wont he became angry at the meat. But then he calmed down. And I think it was on Sunday night, late Sunday night, that he had his insight about why he had been resenting everyone's presence and saying it was amazing how insensitive people could be when actually everyone has been very nice. He suddenly realised that he was actually angry at the foetus and projecting this anger at those around us. Because we've been so happy together and he's afraid the baby will take me away from him.

'Since this insight he's been much happier,' I say brightly, only to go on to report an almost identical incident after a delicious meal he made on Bank Holiday Monday.

Commenting on another row a week or so later, I muse complacently, 'I think it is very hard for men because they have to watch a pregnancy rather than feel it.' As if I could bear to feel it myself!

So the question is: How do you manage to 'think through the body' if what you'd really like to do is escape it? You prepare yourself for childbirth the same way you'd prepare yourself for the trip you wish you were taking instead. You decide where you want to go, and how, and who you want to take with you. You find out as much as you can about your destination, compare and contrast all available forms of accommodation. Just what kind of pain-management are you going to go for? What's your position on foetal monitors, ultrasound, episiotomies? A few months earlier, you didn't even know the words. Now you could write the encyclopaedia. But still you go to class, really for the satisfaction of listening to an expert confirm that you knew everything already. And also for the company, which you crave with a desperation you are reluctant to admit. What a relief to know there are other people out there who have been equally conscientious about eating from all four food-groups, who have come to equally rigid conclusions about the specific way in which they hope to take charge of the birth process. But even with all this solidarity, how hard it is to see eye to eye:

At the end of the class the subject of Leboyer was broached. The physiotherapist, though tolerant in tone, did not think much of him, did not think a bath in water would be all that soothing, thought that waiting for the last pulse to go through the umbilical cord to be potentially unsafe, thought that dim lights could hinder the medical team, etc., etc. But then a few women spoke apprehensively of birth trauma. I asked why it was so bad if birth was a bit of a trauma, the strength to overcome trauma in life being so important. I'm afraid I upset some of them. I feel so bad about this. I think the only one who agreed with me was the deb surgeon's wife. She said to me half-jokingly, 'Like slapping the baby to show it life is cruel,' and I said, 'Yes, I'll slap mine twice so it really gets the message,' but I think this was too harsh for her too. Oh why do I say things like that?

Obviously, because I was getting cold feet. These got colder during the last class:

. . . at which we listened to the long, unfortunate story from a woman who had a last-minute Caesarean. She'd been in hospital since the thirty-fifth week with toxaemia. Labour began in the thirty-seventh week. It went on for eighteen hours, then the baby was in the wrong position, so they tried forceps, unsuccessfully. It turned out that her pelvis was too small. So they did the Caesarean. As she was debilitated and the baby was premature she didn't see it for two days and then had trouble accepting it. But she seemed to have recovered. It was a sombre note on which to end the classes.

I remember this pale, spent woman well. I recall how far away she seemed. How she made the other side of birth sound like the other side of the Styx.

III

Then it was my turn. Let's see, where to take up the story?

Let's start ten days after the due date. Pollyanna is back where we left her, languishing in bed. 'I feel as if I've spent my whole life waiting, waiting – first to get pregnant, and then for this birth.' The mental strain, I now have to admit, was fast becoming unbearable:

> On the one hand, failing to believe labour would ever begin, and on the other, knowing that in a few hours I could easily be writhing in pain on a bed in a delivery room surrounded by strangers.

This was Tuesday afternoon. Tuesday night we went to have dinner with a dear friend whose ne'er-do-well boyfriend had left her:

> She was convinced something was wrong with her, because she couldn't help feeling jealous. She was so desperately unhappy, and convinced she was old, convinced she should try and live a carefree existence. We talked and talked but could hardly get through. It is hard to make someone in love see reason [I sigh condescendingly]. By the time we got home we felt very drained from the strain. I was all tired out, Paul was all wired up. I wanted to go to sleep, Paul wanted to talk. I felt strange, I can't exactly describe how. I had a feeling I was

about to go into labour, but as usual I mistrusted my intuition
. . . Of course I didn't tell him about it until our fight was well
under way.

His feelings were hurt that I kept asking him to shut up
because I didn't want to think about anyone but myself.

The fight that ensued was, I report, the usual one. It ended
when he went to bed because he couldn't go out because I had
hidden his wallet:

I stayed up for another hour and a half feeling very sorry
about my lot, and plotting my revenge for the next day.

At half-past six I awoke feeling pain in my kidneys. [This
turned into contractions.] I tried to time them but Paul's
watch, my watch, and the East German clock all had different
times, so the recording became quite confusing. I watched
Paul sleeping blissfully, thinking: Little does he know.

Soon I had no choice but to let him know, and soon after the
deeply satisfying awakening, we were off to the hospital:

I remember looking at a park in the Euston area feeling very
resigned and ready to take whatever labour had in store for
me. [In front of the hospital] I felt very pathetic with my
suitcase in my hand, knowing that I would eventually come
out that door a different person.

Admission was somewhat brutal in that hospital at that time.
After a 'tortuous' breaking of the waters, and a 'very unpleasant'
enema I was:

. . . dispatched with my shopping trolley to the bathroom.
My contractions were so strong I could barely see straight.
I rushed to the toilet where I sat in great pain, unable to
distinguish the contraction part of it from the enema part
of it. So I got up for my shower too early and had to
leap out of the bathtub halfway through, nearly breaking
my neck.

I remember feeling very lost and confused and convinced that I had taken so long that there was an enormous queue outside the door, and many writhing and furious expectant mothers. What I don't remember is how I got to the labour room. I remember leaning breathlessly against a wall trying to remember how to attach a sanitary towel to a sanitary belt while the contractions came in rapid succession. By the time Paul appeared, I could barely speak. It wasn't the pain that kept me from speaking, it was just that I couldn't spare the energy . . . I had already put my blinkers on. Being in labour is like rushing top-speed down a highway. You can't afford to step and look around. You can only look forward with a concentration that is almost blindness.

I think this was when I let go of the idea that labour was a cultural symbol in need of reshaping:

Paul was, I think, quite shaken by my transformation. He didn't show it. He helped me on to the bed, held my hand, sat down by my side. The bed was quite high, and I remember it was hard, although I've since been told it was soft.

Things got worse over the next four hours or so, despite my failure to withstand the pain without pethidine, and then unbearable when I pushed before the cervix was fully dilated, thereby slowing the process down. For the next forty-five minutes, I was not allowed to push again:

I have never been through anything more excruciating . . . I concentrated on the visual image of swollen cervix lip which grew more swollen every time I wanted to give up and push . . . it was beyond pain. I asked for more pethidine but the midwife said no. I was to use gas and air. Paul stood beside me. Every time a contraction came I would put the mask on and breathe fast enough to set up a rhythm against the contracting womb, which was trying with all its might to eject the baby. As the contractions grew stronger, there was a point in every contraction when the contraction would break my rhythm at which point the midwife and student nurses would start chanting, 'Breathe, breathe, breathe.' Every time the contraction overcame my efforts, I felt a complete failure. If it was so easy, why weren't they doing it?

The Board of Midwives had come to do a surprise inspection of the wards that day, and the student midwives were scurrying from ward to ward to stay out of the dragons' way. Apparently they were appalled by the wish I expressed while 'pushing into pain': 'Let it be a boy so he'll never have to go through this!'

I was under the impression that I was doing a bad job of it, when Paul said, 'You're doing well.' That gave me the strength to go on. Then soon after that they could see the head. I averted my gaze for the episiotomy, and it didn't hurt. Then more contractions, more pushing, a tearing feeling. The midwife went in with her hands, but I don't remember this. All I remember is a baby suddenly shooting out and lying on his back before my eyes. What had been the most excruciating pain of my life suddenly disappeared. I felt great surprise. It was almost as if I had forgotten that the result of all this would be a baby. Then they said, 'It's a boy!' And Paul's voice cracked as he cried, 'A boy!' I felt surprised again, as if I had forgotten that it would either be a girl or a boy.

The baby was brownish purple, with a head moulded into a turban. He cried right away. He looked so perfect to me I didn't even bother to worry about his fingers and toes. I felt so wonderful that I wanted to get up right away.

I had forgotten about the afterbirth.

Selfless

I

When they wheeled me on to the fourth floor I was in a daze, and smiling as if I had just been swept on to a stage to receive a prize, and only vaguely aware that the gigantic bouquet of flowers I was holding was hitting one hospital bed after another. When I walked out of the hospital with

Paul and Matthew a week later I was still in a daze . . . Added to the shock and the euphoria of the birth was now the continuing shock of motherhood. I had been anticipating this violent switch from sluggishness to frenzied activity, but there is no way to prepare yourself.

Almost five months later, 'I have yet to recover fully,' I confess, and then add, in smaller letters: 'Perhaps you never do.'

The hospital policy was to start us looking after our babies 'as soon as you could stagger to the bathroom on your own two feet.' This was good, I thought, because 'the interfering efficiency of any army of nurses' would have only served to fuel my fears.

I had to improvise, and from the moment when I managed against all odds to lift him from the plexiglass trolly, I knew I would be able to take good care of him. I knew he was no china doll and I knew I was his mother.

This does not mean that I was suddenly and serenely in control!

Getting ready to breast-feed was like 'trying to convince myself to jump into icy water'. Changing his nappy was a 'frightening ordeal'. Because there was hardly a time when I wasn't doing the one thing or the other, the days were 'phenomenally exhausting'. The hospital routine 'began at half-past six with a dark hand appearing between the curtains' and continued relentlessly until eleven at night. It was only after-hours that we were allowed to get on with 'the very private, almost secret intercourse between each of us and our babies, the furtive play periods in the dark, the long gazes through the plexiglass . . . while the babies solemnly studied our faces'.

The biggest shock of motherhood was my failure to make sense of it. The pieces didn't fit together. I had no wisdom to fall back on, not even the shadow of a frame of reference. My descriptions of the early days are of highs and lows that I cannot fit together, of old strategies farcically misapplied and described like tragedies.

'The day after the birth I received the proofs of my book,' reads the desperately, wishfully smug conclusion of my pregnancy diary, 'so I know for sure that the satisfaction of seeing your first words in print is nothing, nothing in comparison to seeing your first baby.'

But I do remember that correcting these proofs was like touching base, that the sight of these proofs underneath the pots of flowers and greeting cards was the only reminder I had that, somewhere out there, life as I knew it was continuing, and that one day somehow I would again be part of it. I also remember that even to feel this link seemed like a betrayal of the baby. The only way to make up for this treachery was, of course, to spurn the proofs and put him first. Because of the person I was at the time, this meant treating him like a research project for whom anything less than a perfect mark would mean criminal negligence. Neatly folded into the back of my diary is my hospital feeding-chart, complete with date, time, and how long the baby stayed on which breast. 'Sucked quite well; sucked well,' some official person has written next to the first two entries. In the spaces underneath, I have written:

Hesitated, then sucked well; sucked well; sucked well; sucked well but was angry at the end; sucked too well, occasionally taking in more than he could swallow and then lost interest; sucked well; sucked lethargically; sucked well but intermittently – very drowsy.

I kept up this hysterical excuse for a lab report for weeks, and I take some small comfort in knowing that I wasn't the only one.

There were six of us in the ward. 'For all of us it was the first baby,' I wrote later:

I was the youngest; all the others were thirty-one or thirty-two and all had careers. We were all so relieved to be able to talk without inhibition about our obsessions, all the things we had always found so boring in other obsessed mothers before becoming pregnant ourselves. [I was sure anyone else would have been appalled.] Because so much of our shared experience is beyond the realm of polite conversation – the tenderness of our nipples, the colour and consistency of our babies' bowel movements, how much milk was leaking out of our breasts, progress reports on my stitches. We ourselves felt no embarrassment, only passionate interest. I remember thinking on my last day what an adjustment it would be to remember that people on the outside would not find these topics as interesting.

I end this last attempt at maternal memoir with a morose memory of a midnight feed in the nursery with the woman I had got to know best:

I was in great pain because I had forgotten my rubber ring. Linda was feeding Sean. Because of her engorgement, she had to remove her nightgown from her shoulders in order to feed him and unlace the binding she had to wear around her bust. As he fed from one breast, milk sprayed all over her nightgown (newly bought that afternoon to replace a score of other similarly soaked nightgowns), his legs and vest, the binding and the floor. Then, when she stood up to go get some tissues, her nightgown and binding fell to her feet, leaving her almost naked, with Sean still on one breast and the other breast still emanating milk as efficiently as a sprinkler. We laughed and laughed at the indignity of it all – after all the hard knocks of pregnancy, to have to go through this. I said having a child was one long exercise in self-humiliation. We were feeling exactly the same, our spirits almost broken. We were homesick, euphoric and scared. After so much isolation and loneliness while I was pregnant, it was good to be with people who were facing the same joys and humiliations, even though we all would have preferred to be home.

Later, whenever things went wrong, I would look at our window, the same window at which I had stood and felt I was the only one in the world who was pregnant, and know that over those roofs there was Linda in West Hampstead, Pearl in Golders Green, Ivana in Kentish Town, Nur in Islington, all going through the same thing, all of them obsessed with feeding and changing and rashes and laundry and colic, and all of them reeling from lack of sleep, all of them understanding how caring for an infant was a combination of pure heaven and pure hell.

I'm sure one of the reasons the writing stops here is that I was not equal to the challenge of describing the events that set me moping at the window. That week in hospital, for all its indignities, was the closest I have ever got to a stable environment, and the only time I have ever come close to experiencing the suffocating, routine-led, but reassuringly predictable institution of motherhood as Adrienne Rich described it. When I got home, the institution I was meant to be fighting against was nowhere in evidence. Instead I found Paul valiantly holding to the promise that we had both made and that I had already backed out on. While I hid behind the baby, he continued living by our old bohemian rules.

But how were we to combine that way of life with this colicky baby? Our dilemma became all the more fraught when an ex-boss of mine began turning up at two in the morning with bottles of champagne. And then there was my family. They had all come for Christmas, at my invitation, of course. My mother had wanted to help me, but I was only one of many competing for her time. There were my father's eggs to make in the morning, and his slippers to find, his second, third, fourth coffees to carry to his desk, quickly to be followed by his first, second, third, fourth beers. There was my brother's mattress to inspect for razor blades. He had not yet made a full recovery from the breakdown that had forced him to drop out of college. There was my sister's endometriosis, which led to her being hospitalised. There was her new fiancé, whom I was meeting for the first time, and then, suddenly, there was her old fiancé, who had refused to accept the letter she had sent to him in Germany, and who had now arrived for the festive season along with his mother and his sister.

I understand now why, when my sister was released from hospital on New Year's Eve, she was taking the wisest, and indeed the only sane course, when she decided to drive two hundred miles through a blizzard to meet her future in-laws.

She was not to know that this same blizzard was going to prevent her former fiancé, and his mother, and his sister, from returning to Germany to attend the masked ball that was the social event of the year. Neither was she to know that, at exactly the same time, her two best friends from university were flying across the Atlantic to pay her a surprise visit. My parents felt particularly sorry for the former fiancé's mother, and so they invited her to come along with them to the small dinner party that a dear, recently widowed old friend was throwing for them. They were glad when the fiancé's mother declined, because when my sister's long-lost college friends got in touch, it meant they could offer to take this couple with them instead. My sister's long-lost friends said they would think about it.

When they turned up on our doorstep at eight that evening, it turned out they were not two, but three. When the doorbell rang five minutes later, it was the fiancé's mother who had changed her mind, too – and brought along her children. And then there was my brother, who was not looking well enough to be left on his own. My parents' dear, recently widowed friend was expecting two people for supper. When my parents set out for her house, I counted nine. My parents were so embarrassed that, after they rang their friend's doorbell, they hid behind a column. When the friend answered the door, and saw in front of her seven people she didn't recognise, she thought they were carol singers. Dinner was Shrimps Newburg. They got one-and-a-half shrimps each.

In retrospect, it is not surprising to me that I did not have enough breast milk. I do not know what I would have done without my kindly health visitor. She was a godsend after the district midwife, whose first act had been to sterilise a pair of scissors, asked me to open my legs so that she could get rid of those disgusting stitches, and told me, when I balked at the suggestion, that she did not believe I was the one to have given birth to this baby. But the health visitor was all tact and empathy. She came over for a friendly visit, and a teeny tiny whisky, last thing every evening. Eventually, and in a very roundabout way, she talked me out of those feeding-charts and into an approach that was more relaxed and intuitive. She gave me a book called *Breast is Best*. It was very informative without ever commanding a set course from on high. I did not realise then how rare a compliment this was. When, seven weeks after the birth, for reasons too complicated to explain and even harder for me to understand now, I found myself eight time-zones away, in El Paso, Texas, living with my mother-in-law, I came to use this book – quite literally – as a shield.

By four months, the baby weighed 16 lbs, but at two months, he still weighed only 8, which was below his birth weight. So naturally, my mother-in-law was worried, especially when I developed mastitis and a 104° temperature. She got me straight to the doctor – something I could not have done alone, as I could not drive, and something Paul could not have done either, as he was in New York looking for work. My mother-in-law's nursing skills left something to be desired. She didn't believe in fresh food. I made do with hot liquids and kept the baby on the breast for as long as possible while I read my new bible. My mother-in-law didn't approve. In her day, breast had been thought of as worst, and nothing could come near a baby unless it had been sterilised. She didn't think I was 'careful' enough, and she didn't think much of the sterilisation tablets I had brought with me from England. She thought they were responsible for Matthew's low weight. I kept her at bay by waving *Breast is Best* at her and saying I was following its instructions. This bought me space and time but not her confidence. After all, it was a British book, 'And I don't truly believe they know what they're talking about, especially when it comes to the kind of microbes we have in the desert.'

She didn't like some of the dangerous habits I had brought with me from London – like taking the baby into bed for feeds, and picking him up every time he cried. And she was appalled at some of the safety measures I was unwilling to adopt – like bed clamps to keep him from kicking off his blankets when he cried in his cot, and washing the entire house down every day in disinfectant, and wearing a surgical mask while breast-feeding. In her opinion, I was just not up to the job. The first thing she would do in the morning was stand at the doorway to the bedroom, look at me and the nursing baby, shake her head, and say, 'He's not going to make it.'

In a state of emergency boundaries count for very little. Fighting for my life at this point and fighting for his life were one and the same. I can look back now and remember not just the struggle but what I learned by going through it. I can see that, if it hadn't been this particular struggle, it would have been another one, given my *laissez-faire* optimism and appalling ignorance. I wouldn't like to go through it again, but since I did get through it, and since the baby did, too, I can afford to be thankful for the experience. I went into it a snivelling blob who had to concentrate to digest an egg and couldn't think beyond the next banana. I came out of it with the vaguest hint of an understanding about what it meant to take responsibility for someone who did not fall under the heading 'My Body, Myself'.

When I think back on this more heroic former self, I want to give her a medal. I want her to look around her and congratulate herself for managing to keep a baby alive and well while navigating through such craziness. Alas, I could not appreciate my accomplishments at the time. I was too busy worrying that I had fallen into that dread state that for millennia had turned women from free agents into the willing pawns of patriarchy. Selflessness.

II

After I had committed *Breast is Best* to memory, I moved on, I remember, to Doris Lessing's 'Children of Violence' series. I think it was the name that attracted my horror and therefore my interest. (It is probably no accident that the other book next to my bed was called *Children of Crisis*.) The second volume of Doris Lessing's quartet is the ultimate story of a mother fending off selflessness. Martha Quest has married a dull, Rhodesian businessman and has been forced into the circumscribed conventions of bourgeois city life. Unable to exercise her mind or act on her convictions, she is deprived even of an opportunity to bond with her infant daughter. Truby King, the baby doctor everyone was meant to obey during the thirties, held the view that babies from birth on suffered irreparable damage unless their mothers kept them in their cots twelve hours a night and declined during that time to feed them. After listening to her baby cry non-stop night after night, Martha's ultimate, and almost involuntary, response is to leave.

I was horrified. Although the day would come when I, too, would have to leave home, albeit temporarily, at this point I was convinced that I would never, ever abandon a child, even if it meant annihilating my soul.

What did that say about me? I wondered, but asked no one. I asked no one because I spent all but an hour or two of my days alone with the baby. By now we had moved into one of Paul's mother's ranch houses. I would get up at five, watch the morning news programmes, break during the soaps to give Matthew a bath, then give him as many feeds as possible so that I could read as much as possible. Paul would get up at a godlier hour, and then work until suppertime, after which I would collapse into bed, and he would stay up alone watching television.

The worst part of the day was mid-afternoon. It was mid-afternoon when I finished reading the second 'Martha Quest' book. I remember suddenly needing some air. Forgetting where I was, I decided I could benefit from a brisk walk. I put Matthew into his pushchair and out we went into our blighted desert suburb, past the houses with Tudor doors and adobe garages, and cactus gardens, and gnome-studded astroturf lawns, past the street signs featuring misspelt heroes from Greek and chivalric legends, past purring cars and howling dogs, but never past a single human being. And I remember thinking: It's happened. I've fallen off the edge of the earth. I've been expelled from the real world. I've become selfless.

How had I allowed this to happen? Now that I had identified the horrible truth, what was I to do to fight it?

I decided I had to find a way of being selfish. But what exactly did this mean?

I had no idea, so over the frantic weeks that followed I tried every feasible type of selfishness I could think of. I went to the mall by myself. I took a driving lesson. I bought myself a new bathing suit, an overpriced yoghurt, ran up a large phone bill. When nothing did the trick, I asked myself why. Another thing I couldn't understand was why I could not stop myself from continuing to perform the babycare tasks which I was now beginning to see as acts of self-sacrifice, and, it therefore followed, of moral cowardice. It was as if my own mother had come to stay in my head, and was telling my arms and legs what to do. How did she come to have such control over my behaviour, I asked myself. Why am I so beholden to tradition? Where did I go wrong?

The inevitable conclusion was that it was impossible to have a child without feeling this way, without turning into this nonentity. That I ought to have realised this, that I set out on this course too hastily, that I was stuck with my mistakes, that I didn't deserve better anyway, that there was obviously something wrong with me if I had let myself in for this. It was, as my friend Joey likes to put it, a no-win situation that I had no right to complain about. So I kept my guilt-ridden anger inside and smouldering. And looked for a scapegoat. Conveniently forgetting that I no longer even dreamed of keeping my promise about earning half the money, I turned my attention to the man who had fallen way short of his promise to be an equal parent. Who had broken a sacred promise, I now decided, and who in so doing was condemning me to a life of servitude.

Man as other

All men are rapists. That's a useful thing to know when you're eighteen, afraid and in need of a motto that will serve as an amulet. Every rule has its exceptions, and so it doesn't surprise you that you happen to know so many of them. You're just unbelievably lucky to be surrounded by these rare gems, men who aren't necessarily rapists. At the same time your trust for your father, your brother, the one teacher who seems to treat you like a human being, is made just a little fragile by your reluctance to test it. You're careful, too, in other ways — particularly with regard to your boyfriend, that ultimate cipher with whom you are often alone in a room. You are not entirely convinced about his many obvious weaknesses. You know how quickly sexism can rear its head, and you know, also, about how susceptible you are to affections that may not be in your best interests. You're unpleasantly aware that feminism as you know it and men as you desire them are puzzle-pieces that refuse to interlock. But if you don't really have the will to give up your ideals for love, or to forgo male company for your ideals, you try not to think about it.

You set your sights on the man who is an exception even in the company of exceptions. Otherwise, how could you justify the ever-increasing number of ways in which you bow to tradition? This man in your bed, not only does he *never presume* – he cooks every other night, takes out the rubbish, and loves you first and foremost for your mind. There's another story, too, the florid nightmare that rises like a rainbow over every domestic cloud. It goes like this: you've been duped. He doesn't believe in equal partnership for a second. He tricks you into submission. He goes into a sulk if you don't thank him every time he lifts a finger. This is the story that you take away from every disappointment and bleat out tearfully to friends in exchange for similar confessions. If you get back together with its villain, you need to convince yourself that you were exaggerating, that the truth must lie somewhere between the two stories. But the pendulum never stops swinging long enough for you to figure out exactly where.

Saints and devils. Madonnas and whores. Subjects and objects. Selves and others. A quarter-century of feminist critique has devoted itself to examining the patriarchal bent for split visions. The premise is that the problem is in the eye of the beholder. If a man looks at a woman and sees either vice or virtue personified, he is not seeing her at all, he is seeing a projection of his ideas. Or to be precise, half of his ideas. He is seeing either one half of a contradiction, or the other. He cannot bear to see both at the same time, because then he'd have to admit that there is something wrong with the way he sees things.

But then again, neither can I, and for the same reason. When my ideals and my experience conflict, I am far more likely to be guided by the former. The known world is what they illuminate well. Anything they cannot illuminate is a mystery. Is not part of the known world. Is the Other. Is, in other words, almost always a man. This man is at his most mysterious when he makes his appearance in the traditionally female world. And of all the forms this changeling has been known to take, the most enigmatic of them all is the Post-natal Father.

It began in the labour ward. It began with a look. A wild, lingering look that did not quite match what he said: that for the first time in his life, he respected women for what they had to go through. It betrayed a deep, deep anxiety, and it only went away when it was he who was holding the baby, not I. This was the only time when he looked the way I wanted him to. This was the look I tried to freeze on film. Only to see that wild, lingering, and yes, reproachful look return when I asked him to adjust his elbow. The baby's head was too low, I told him. But there was something about the way he changed his pose that reminded me of the way he once behaved when I explained to him why the words '*Je veux*' must be followed by the word '*que*' if you are intending to use the subjunctive.

What's going on, I asked myself. But then he smiled, well, it was more like a fierce glare, for the camera, and I caught it on film. The proud pose lasted for as long as peace lasted. Then the baby made a noise, a damp patch suggested itself, an alarm went off in his eyes. The first time this happened there was an uncertainty about the way he offered the baby. It was a question, a deference to authority. Do you want to take care of this one, or shall I? This is a tricky one for the new mother who so believes politics reside in domestic details, but who has zero knowledge of how to perform those domestic details. It is especially so if the test case is breast-fed. Asking a man to take equal care of a breast-fed newborn baby is asking him to change all the nappies. Which didn't seem fair, it now occurred to me. Or the best way to get a father and a baby to bond. If they were going to bond, they ought to be getting to know each other in more pleasant surroundings. If their only point of contact was the changing table, things could go very wrong. Which is why, when he offered me the baby that first time, I said no darling, don't worry. I'll take care of this one.

And when I was halfway through taking care of this one, and

looked up to see if he was watching, I mistook his fixed stare for rapt attention. I thought he was studying my movements so as to master the task. So I was shocked when, the next time he was holding the baby, and the baby indicated an urgent need, he handed the bundle over to me as automatically as if I had pressed a button. As I struggled through the unfamiliar motions under his see-through gaze, I strained to see things from his point of view — to understand his feelings. I concluded that, if I had had a choice in the matter, I too would be pretty quick to hand the bundle over. What bothered me, really, was the speed of the handover. It was so clear that he hasn't even paused to consider my feelings, let alone the larger issues of bonding. All he was doing was trying to get out of an unpleasant job. How to make sense of this? I asked myself as he passed, practically hurled, the bundle back into my arms. The baby's cries interrupted this train of thought. The baby needed a change, and until he was changed, all other matters had to wait. I became lost in the task. Lost because inept. I just didn't have the hang of it yet. I had to go through four, five, six nappies before I managed to get one on right, and the whole time this was going on, my presumed equal partner watched with a dropped jaw and with his arms dangling lifelessly at his sides. Maybe he's just scared, I thought. Then I thought: But I'm scared, too.

I thought, but I did not dare say, because the most terrifying thing of all was the thought that neither of us was up to the challenge. And yet we were going to have to rise to it.

'He came after lunch,' I wrote about the day we went home from hospital:

> He had a suitcase full of clothes for me and Matthew. I had already assembled the carrycot. But then came the almost insurmountable challenge of dressing Matthew. How to put on a Curity Snuggler nappy? How to push his flailing arms through the narrow sleeves of a babygro? His arms only filled half the sleeves. He suddenly looked so small and lost.
>
> Outside London looked beautiful. Matthew went to sleep in the car. All the way home, I was in seventh heaven. The cab driver, taking advantage of the situation, took the long way and overcharged us. When we got home, Paul walked the

baby while I tried to find some clothing I could feed Matthew in. After I had fed him, we put him into his beautiful wicker bassinet that the Goodwins had lent us. We sat on the bed in seventh heaven. Matthew made a few little sounds. We had arrived, I felt. Then Matthew began to cry. I fed him a little more. He shat all over his blue babygro. It was a shock to us that the Curity Snuggler could not contain the shit within its boundaries. We decided it was low quality. We took out all the other types of disposable nappies and rubber pants. They were all too big except one. I put the changing mat on the bed and began to change him. While he was uncovered (and screaming) he pissed all over the bed and the wall. I remember a high and wavering arc of urine. Paul rushed to get the Kleenex and tripped over my open suitcase. We both became hysterical. The honeymoon was over, and the ordeal had begun.

But the thing I couldn't understand was why it wasn't the same ordeal for both of us.

Our lives continued to diverge. This was all the more mysterious as we were still sharing the same small spaces and revolving around the same all-important baby. It was as if we were using the same stage to obey two different scriptwriters. Mine – it gradually dawned on me – called for me to be perpetually on call. His, I now realise, called for him to take care of absolutely everything else so that I could be perpetually on call. But that's not how I saw it at the time. In my new hell of interrupted sleep all I could see was that he got more sleep than I did, and had more freedom of movement than I did.

What I saw was that he didn't respond to things the same way I did. Where I saw a crying baby that needed picking up, or a pile of laundry that needed folding, or a wastepaper basket that was filled to the brim, he seemed to see a blank wall. The more truncated my nights became, the more important it was to him to get a full night's sleep. The greater the gap between the time I woke up and the time he woke up, the more reluctant he was to admit that the gap even existed.

As arguments gave way to silent, one-sided conversations, anger turned into soul-searching. I convinced myself I was doing something wrong. My anger and envy did not quite mesh with the fact that, actually, holding the baby was also a source of pride and intense pleasure. I had never quite acknowledged that what I resented his not doing were the very tasks that not even a dog from hell would have induced me to share with him. That what I was asking him – and asking in a shamelessly hypocritical manner – was impossible. You can't take responsibility without having any responsibilities. You can't think and act like a primary carer if you're not a primary carer. It was a doomed exercise.

I had not seen this until now because until now I had had only one question for such matters: Who's in control? The reason I depended on this two-dimensional measurement of power is that every feminist book I had ever so much as browsed through depended on it, too. But the old formula didn't work any more. In this context, it was nonsense.

Who *was* in control in this context – the one, the other, or the baby? If control meant that you could get other people to do all the work, then, clearly, it was the baby. But that couldn't be so, could it, as the baby was also helpless. It had to be the mother who was in control, because she was the one who was in charge of looking after the baby, and she was the one whose decision was almost always final.

But what a price she had to pay for her position of authority! Nothing less than perpetual servitude. Nothing less than the perpetual headache of having to put someone else's needs first. Not that she, I, wanted to complain too much, because she, I, had come to love this small tyrant whose life depended on her, my, clumsy ministrations. I had to admit it – the greater the inroads the baby made on my freedom, the more powerful I felt and was.

And it wasn't a one-way street either. I was learning from the baby just as much as the baby was learning from me. This baby, although physically helpless, had a will, and a personality. Taking care of him was never so straightforward as learning to fill needs. Guesswork was involved. You tried everything you could think of until you found something that worked. In other words, you were using your mind, coming to your own conclusions, and acting on them. In other words, I was not living as stupid or as passive a life as people seemed to think. In fact, I was in control of my life. And the baby's life. And as the months passed, I had managed to create out of chaos an intermittently pleasing and harmonious routine. My life with the baby was taking shape. My life had purpose.

I became convinced that, if I asked Paul who was in control, he would answer without hesitation that it was I. It was I because I was running the whole show. I was the one who decided when and how to care for the baby. I set the agenda, and he had to fit in with it. The hardest thing for him had to be that he couldn't even complain about it. Because if he did, I would ask him the obvious question, which was how could I possibly be in control if I couldn't even take a bath without asking him to hold the baby?

But I *was* in control, I now realised. My power was all the greater for my insistence that I didn't have any. I decided to be more understanding. If I put myself in his shoes occasionally, then I could keep myself from acting like a typical traditional mother and stop undermining him.

By now Matthew was eight months old. We had moved to San Francisco, a few hundred yards from one of Paul's best friends, and a mile or so away from another. Both friends were single. They liked to go out a lot. As did Paul. Sometimes, if I had advance notice, I did. More often than not, there was a problem with babysitters. There were very few I would trust, and even these chosen ones were only to be trusted at times when the baby was asleep. I ended up spending many evenings at home alone with the baby. As I sat there, suppressing my rage, and trying to figure out where the hell Paul's shoes were so that I could imagine I was standing in them, the baby and I got very close. By now breast-feeding had gone from something akin to jumping into icy water to a pleasure that I was beginning to suspect was almost sexual.

I convinced myself that this was the crux of the problem. Paul was going out more and more because he felt more and more excluded. He would only come back if the situation changed. For the situation to change, I was going to have to make a sacrifice. I took Matthew off the breast and put him on the bottle.

I waited for the situation to change.

It didn't.

Pacing my cage night after night, less and less able to contain my rage, I counted the ways in which Paul had betrayed me.

But by the time I worked up the courage to demand that he put more time in, give the baby breakfast every other day, and on alternate days, do supper or bathtime, all thought of gender formation had gone out of the window. All I wanted was to punish him. Knock him into shape.

And I did. Before long, the savage was housetrained. He even took pleasure in it. In time, there were many things he was convinced that he did better than I! I grew to resent this. Our sharing of care was pockmarked with arguments about how much bubble bath to put into the water, how long to steam the vegetables, how much to dilute the apple juice. There were times when I was glad Matthew and I still had the vast days to ourselves. I was almost glad that Paul was still going out at night. At the same time I bitterly resented the fact that I was left holding the baby.

Get a babysitter, Paul said, when I complained. But who would I ever trust to treat Matthew right when he was awake? Why was I so untrusting? What was wrong with me? Why had I turned into my own worst enemy? Why such a failure at equal parenting? And the worst part of it was I was not just falling into a trap that would ruin *my* life and prospects, I was, by bringing up a son in a way that was ever more traditional, perpetuating all the worst evils of Western civilization.

And not just doing it in thousands of little everyday unwitting ways. Doing it deliberately! When I dutifully gave Matthew a doll for his first birthday, I was superficially flustered, but deeply, deeply pleased, to watch him use it like a torpedo. It was just what I would have liked to have done to certain people's heads.

And that was terrible, terrible. Here Paul was, doting on his son now every other day at breakfast, and on alternate days doting over him during bath or suppertime, and every day my thoughts towards him were more and more murderous. How could this be when I loved him? Why did I long to get away from my baby when I wouldn't even stoop to the idea of a babysitter? Why was I failing?

Then I found out that everyone else was, too.

5

OTHER MOTHERS

Into the ghetto

One Sunday afternoon two summers before I had Matthew, I had the misfortune of finding myself stranded inside a group of new mothers. It was a barbecue for the crew and cast of a Monty Python movie. The new mothers were their wives, but I couldn't figure out why because they were the most stultifying people I had ever met. From the moment they spread themselves and their cumbersome equipment over the lawn, until the moment they began the arduous job of 'picking up their bits and pieces', they did nothing but discuss pyjama sizes. Which ones had snaps? Which ones flameproof treatment? What happened if you used ordinary detergent on materials thus treated? Who had the most darling styles for babygros? The most reliable sizing chart? And how about sleepsuits? When was the right time to move a toddler from the ones with feet to the ones without feet and did anyone know of a brand that came in small sizes that had feet that could fold back into nifty padded cuffs? I remember the amorous intensity with which they locked eyes, the way they froze their pert little faces whenever someone offered up an exciting new tidbit. They were like sparrows eyeing a worm. As I sat there listening in vain for some hint that I was watching a parody in action, some confirmation that what I was watching was an elaborate joke, I vowed to myself that, if I ever had children, I would never ever ever allow myself to sink to the discussion of pyjama sizes.

After Matthew was born, the drawing of the line between Them and Me became more emphatic. Having failed as a body politician and as an equal parent, having succumbed against my will to symptoms of selflessness, I was hysterically determined to save myself from the mother-and-child ghetto. One of the early lies I told myself was that I had enjoyed the society of other mothers in hospital because they were as eager to avoid this ghetto as I was. We had all worked before pausing to have children. We would go back to work in due course. As obsessed as we all were with the minutiae of babycare, we still read our newspapers first thing in the morning. If I had remained in London, if I had been able to keep in touch with these exceptional beings with whom I had been lucky enough to share a maternity ward, I might have been able to drift into the maternal network without even realising what was happening. And, after a time, I might have been able to pick up a book about the mother–child dyad and its effect on gender formation, or an article referring to the mother-and-child ghetto, and been able to see the picture they painted as a nightmare scenario that bore no resemblance to my life.

But as I did not stay in London, I had to overcome my feminist prejudices about mothers, children, and ghettos the hard way. This was partly to do with my own snobberies, partly to do with the fact that the mothers and children I had occasion to observe, from a petrified and ambivalent distance, first in El Paso, and then in San Francisco, did seem to conform to that nightmare scenario. They also made me feel like an alien. Every time I let my standards down and fell into conversation with these women, some terrible chasm would emerge that made a second conversation unthinkable.

In El Paso, I made the mistake of talking to a woman across the street who had a baby a few months older than Matthew. The next day, she invited me to a Tupperware party. A Tupperware party! Against my better judgement, I accepted. I think I was hoping there would be someone else there whose attitude might be politely ironic. But no, they all took it as seriously as the hostess. I slunk away after making what I hoped was the minimum purchase. The last time I saw the hostess was when she delivered my two sandwich crispers. Unaware of the depth of my snobbery, she asked me if I would like to come over sometime to see a cute children's clothing catalogue a friend had just sent her. It contained some darling pyjamas, she told me. I was on the phone at the time to a gay friend from college. He laughed and laughed and laughed about how far I had fallen.

I didn't speak to another mother until we were living in San Francisco and Matthew was eight months old. This woman's baby was two months old. She and her husband maintained yachts for a living. After a promising conversation about breast-feeding, I invited her back to our apartment for a coffee. I ought to have heard alarm bells when she said, actually, she was against coffee, and would prefer herbal tea. I also ought to have enquired further about her ambition to devote herself full time in future to the Hunger Project, which was an offshoot of est that aimed to end world hunger by a set date, not by putting money into food projects, but by putting money into public relations. I ought to have known we would not see eye to eye about anything except breast-feeding, and perhaps, if I had dared to broach the subject, pyjama sizes. I ought to have given some weight to her claim that her first two months of motherhood had progressed without a single negative feeling. Everything had been going beautifully, she told me, because she had prepared herself mentally and physically for the challenge as well as cultivating the right attitude. But in my isolation I was losing my social graces. As we sipped our herbal teas, I found myself blurting out an assortment of miserable confessions about men, birth, boredom, sleep-deprivation, and enforced solitude. The next time I saw this woman, she pretended not to see me, made an abrupt about turn, and scurried around the nearest corner.

For a week or so, I cried. Then I decided to work with what I had. Execute my duties honourably, cultivate the right attitude. Every afternoon, when Matthew woke up from his nap, I would put him into his pushchair, point him into a different direction from the day before, and then walk two hours before turning round. I found we were both more cheerful afterwards – it seemed that he was as tired as I was of all those days we had spent doing very little while staring into each other's eyeballs. In the course of our walks, I came across ads for various mother-and-baby activities. I decided these were necessary for his development even though I also realised that they would mean intellectual death for me. It was in a spirit of worthy self-sacrifice that I signed us up for all of them.

And they confirmed my worst suspicions – these mothers that I went on to join at Little Flippers, Baby Gym, and Child Observation Class. They were obsessed with the trappings of babycare – not just the pyjamas and the toys and the pushchairs, although helpful hints about these came up with regularity, but also with the neatest recipes for nutritious snacks that did not require mucus-forming ingredients like wheat flour, the best way to deal with infant dental health, the pros and cons of edible Playdo. And childcare books. Why Dr Spock was too bossy, and Berry Brazelton too general, and Penelope Leach too ignorant about food values, and how inadequate they felt after measuring their own children's accomplishments against the developmental charts in The First Twelve Months of Life. Yak yak yak. They couldn't stop complaining, and they had no shame. All the teacher had to do was raise her hand like a conductor and they were off, doing the hokey-cokey, singing 'Dinah, Won't You Blow Your Horn', or 'The Wheels on the Bus Go Round and Round' with all the right hand-gestures.

There seemed to be no limit to the amount of time they were willing to devote to delving into routine childcare issues: how to get a child to sleep through the night, how to handle aggression and tantrums, how to fend off eating disorders and sibling rivalry. The worst part of it was as time wore on, my own interest in these conversations outgrew my ability to turn my back on them. As my standards dropped, these other mothers started looking normal to me. Sometimes I even admired their clothes. Even – although I did not dare stoop to asking where they had bought them – their children's clothes!

I began to join in, even to suppress or soften those opinions that might lead to my quick exclusion. Then I began to see some of these women out of classroom hours. In the beginning the vetting process that ensued was reassuringly painful. It seemed impossible to speak to another mother on a one-to-one basis without having to hear a second-by-second account of her always traumatic labour. But then I grew to enjoy the luxury of repeating my own saga every time someone new asked me over. As my pool of horror stories grew larger, I was able to converse with highbrow enthusiasm about the patterns that were emerging.

I was not the only failure. I had simply failed in my own way. To my great relief, there seemed to be no end to the possibilities when it came to birth failure. No two women had used the same method, medium, position, or location, but all spoke with shaky voices about their shock at losing control, not just of their bodies, but of their thoughts and their emotions. All had at some point had to cede power to a doctor or a hospital authority. All felt like failures – some because they had had Caesareans, some because they had not managed to breathe in a way to make labour painless and had in a moment of weakness cried out for painkillers. One had ruined her perfect home birth by falling head-over-heels in love with the paediatrician who came to visit only hours afterwards.

All of us had gone on to cope badly with breast-feeding, nappy-sharing, housework, lack of sleep, and surfeits of mothers-in-law. All of us felt torn between our reluctance to let any other human being hold our babies, and our ever more urgent resentment about all the things we could no longer do now that we were stuck holding the baby. All of us were shocked, mystified, betrayed, by the babies' fathers when they didn't do enough, and outraged at their presumptions when they did.

If we were all having the same problems, then perhaps we were not looking at personal failures any more, but at unrealistic expectations. As our pained and uncertain confessions accumulated, the questions we asked became more general. Instead of blaming ourselves for not having presided over our bodies heroically, we began to ask: Why so much emphasis on birth, so little preparation for the child that resulted? Why body politics, and why stressing the event over which you are least likely to be able to be presiding genius? Instead of feeling guilty about the uncomfortable blend of love and resentment towards our babies, we began to ask if this wasn't normal. And instead of feeling betrayed by a single man, instead of asking ourselves if we hadn't made a tragically bad choice of partner, we began to ask why all these partners had so much in common.

There were times when we wondered if we weren't all married to the *same* man. They were not doing the amount of childcare they had promised to do. They almost never offered. They had to be asked, and there was a sense that it had to be in the right tone of voice. For what little they did, they expected huge praise. If they did take over a task they enjoyed, they quickly became overbearing, insisting that whatever method they were using was vastly superior to your method. From then on, whenever you were performing this task, they made a point of telling you how stupid you were for doing it your way. Despite this interference, they were willing to go to any lengths to defend their right to come and go, and sleep and work as they pleased.

It took days and days of brutal negotiation and counter-negotiation to change the division of duties, but victory came with a terrible price. When you forced these men to do more than they thought was fair, the really bad apples actually went so far as to feign incompetence. You told them to watch the child when they wanted to read the paper, and you came back to find the child standing on the stove, trying to fit his head into a plastic bag, chewing a pair of scissors. Or worse: one new friend who left her child in the father's care while she went to the bathroom had returned to find her baby floating face down in the swimming pool. Even the good fathers, the ones like Paul who had safety sense, and a knowledge of nutrition, the ones who took the initiative, the ones who actually sat down with their children and read them books – even these wouldn't be caught dead doing all the little extra things that made the difference between a good day and a bad day. They expected the children to take care of themselves while they read the paper. And if you made an issue out of it, they went from feigned incompetence to malevolent interference. They bought their children forbidden substances like chocolate. Dangerous substances like popcorn. And toys with loaded messages, like miniature soldiers, and bath toys that looked like submachine guns. And all this was before you made even the first move to go back to work.

These men had all been as keen on equal parenting as we had been. What had happened? As my new friends and I pushed our pushchairs furiously from playground to playground, we tried to fathom the mystery that was ruining our lives. We discussed what our bottom lines were — how much we were willing to put up with for how long. We drew up strategies. We reported back to each other about tactics that had and hadn't worked, celebrated together over the few victories that did not prove pyrrhic. We resolved not to let our joint defeats break our spirits. Being a mother, we decided, meant finding out how to work with adversity, how to belong to the world even if the world didn't want us. We found that the best way of making that point, to ourselves if to no one else, was to team up and take six or seven toddlers at a time to restaurants that were not accustomed to children. While they played with their food and threw most of it on the floor, and while we picked the food up and apologised to the waiters, the other mothers and I continued our ever more engrossing struggle to define our new condition.

We got so good at carrying out a conversation that we could sometimes finish on Friday a sentence that had been interrupted by a request for juice on Tuesday.

And so it was that one day I found myself sitting in a San Francisco park with a psychologist, a commercial artist, a flight attendant, a secretary, a banker, and two teachers who were now changing careers — one went on to become a public defender, the other to start a children's clothing mail-order company.

They were all in seminar mode, listening with furrowed brows, pursed lips and chins propped up with index fingers, while I expostulated on the differences between British and American pyjama sizes.

I remember catching myself mid-sentence, and thinking: I can't believe I'm doing this, but then persisting anyway. I had a point to make.

The problem as we saw it

The problem as we saw it was that the pyjamas didn't fit. If it said twelve months on the label, you learned eventually that it was hardly large enough for a four month old. If you had a large nine month old, you were lucky if you could squeeze him into pyjamas designed for a toddler. Eventually, you caught on, of course, but it went without saying that anyone who sent me a gift got it horribly wrong. During my time alone, I had convinced myself that I was specially cursed. After I joined the network, I found out that even mothers of small babies had the same trouble. This made us wonder where the official sizing chart came from, and how often it was updated. We cared not because of the pyjamas themselves but because, for the first time in our lives, we had ourselves been forced into a mould that had been designed for a different age and a different kind of mother.

Despite all our efforts to take birth and our bodies back from the doctors, despite all our work to turn the men we lived with into equal parents, despite the ideals we had acquired in the course of our educations, despite our determination not to waste those educations, the world still showed no sign of making room for us. We did not have to imagine the institutional barriers as we had rarely gone outside for a year or more without a child preceding us in a pushchair. Our days consisted of kerbs that were too high, doors that were too narrow, buses that would not wait for us to gather up our equipment, and restaurants that didn't have highchairs. Our futures were clouded by working hours inimical to children's needs, daycare centres that were too impersonal, untrained babysitters who might be better at the work than we were, but who did not necessarily speak English and were more likely than not to be undocumented workers, nursery schools that only served mothers who worked part time because they would not keep children longer than half a day.

But we were convinced that, if we pooled our resources, we'd have no trouble making it change. This, we decided, was the great feminist battle. Not the body, not the birth canal, not the perfect yin and yang kitchen, but the reorganisation of home and work. So the question came to centre on ends and means. What did we want? And how were we going to go about getting it? What kind of balance were we after? If one thing didn't work, then what did we try next? Which experts had ideas that might be useful? Which were too bossy to be believed?

It was in this type of informal, movable symposium that the overabundance of said experts became a boon. One by one, we tore them apart, tested their ideas against our experiences, developed our own ideas, then refined them through trial and error. Selma Fraiberg was right up to a point, but ... Betty Friedan made the mistake of ... those new, non-sexist childcare manuals were so obsessed with chore-sharing that they forgot ... How could you respect a doctor who ... How could you even listen to a political commentator who ... Let alone vote for a sexist who ... We were doing what most experts, including most feminist experts, still believe mothers can't do, which is to think politically.

Although one thing ought to have been clearer to us. Because we were following the same ideas, and sharing notes and supporting our friends, we had this idea that we were acting collectively. While we did our bit to bring about social change, we assumed that our great feminist thinkers and activists were working hard to follow up our efforts with legal and political change. These were the days when there was still lots of fine talk about Equal Rights Amendments and Equal Opportunities Commissions. Because the rhetoric was all about championing a woman's right to work, we assumed they were talking about all women, including us. We also assumed that anyone who championed our right to work was naturally interested in making sure we worked under humane conditions, and that our dependants received adequate care while we did.

What we didn't realise was what equal rights legislation really means. It sets out to erase the legal distinctions between men and women. It is historically against any measures to protect the special needs deriving from pregnancy and maternity because it sees such measures as discriminatory. This means that equal rights campaigns, as they are structured today, are predisposed to ignore not just the differences between men and women, but also the differences between men and women's traditional work. This puts their proponents at odds with women like us who give importance to this work. It is hard for them to understand why we might want to be part of the traditionally male workforce while remaining unwilling to throw our traditionally female responsibilities out of the window.

We didn't realise this, but even if we had, we probably would have gone ahead anyway. At that point in our lives, in that particular group, work was not a necessity but a privilege and a duty. We were out to conquer and alter the workplace on behalf of all women everywhere, to make it adjust to the needs of the mothers who would come after us.

Huh! What a joke.

6

HOME AND WORK

Another confession

I

I remember the expression on my mother's face when I told her – before Matthew was born – that I was going to find new ways of being a mother that would allow me to work. Of course I didn't say it like that. I didn't want her to construe any disapproval on my part for the sacrifices she herself had made to bring children up the old way. I must have said something like, 'Even after the baby's born, I want to keep using my brain.'

She pursed her lips, I remember, only releasing her breath as her eyes slid their true expression under a glaze. 'Aha,' she said after a long pause. 'And are you planning to work out of the house or at home?' 'At home,' I answered, 'at least for the time being.' Another pause. Then, when the sunny smile was back in place, she said, 'I see. But do you think you are going to be able to take a few days off?' 'Oh, of course,' I answered. 'I'm not going to rush. I'll ease back into it. We have enough money to last for at least two months.' Another cloud, another pause, and then: 'Do you think you'll start off working nights?' My answer was that I wasn't going to be rigid about it. 'The whole point of going into writing instead of one of the professions was so that I wouldn't have to adjust to someone else's schedule. I'm going to find my own way. But sensibly. I'll start out by making good use of the baby's naptimes.'

How did my mother feel behind her tactful smile? This is the long, painful story of how I found out. It has never been my mother's habit to share her thoughts, you see. Instead she adds to them by playing the perfect listener. Having entered the new information into her data base, she measures the gap between what you want and what everyone else needs from you, predicts an outcome, and then either herds you quietly in the direction of success or prepares to become the cushion for your disaster. 'I always knew you could do it,' she tells you afterwards. Or 'I was always afraid this would happen. But don't worry. You'll have another chance. In the meantime, sit down, relax, let me make you a nice grilled cheese sandwich.'

Outside the kitchen, my mother is tact and submission and social grace personified. But when she's standing over the stove, she makes fun of everyone and everything. Not only is she one of the world's great mimics – she also encouraged my sister and brother and me to follow in her footsteps. But only when no one was looking, only when we were in the kitchen watching her cook.

The kitchen is her kingdom, and not just anyone is allowed to be her courtier. My father, for example, has no idea what goes on in there. Mystified and attracted by the gales of laughter, he pads out of his study to find out what the joke is. But by the time he arrives, no one can remember it. 'What time is supper?' he asks forlornly. 'Whenever you would like to have it, dear,' my mother says. My father knows, and has been allowed to learn, nothing about cooking. After forty-five years of marriage, he still can't understand why she can't give him a precise prediction for suppertime. It's as if, my mother said once, it's as if he thinks you press a button and presto, the rice is done. This comment has become a joke command for anyone who is having to accede to an unreasonable request: 'What's wrong with you? Get in there and press the rice button!'

When I was a toddler, a very loud toddler who got a big kick out of pushing and shoving, my mother's friends used to ask her what she was going to do to curb my aggression. She says that she thought about it and then decided to do nothing. And the pattern was set. From then on I had permission to do what she didn't dare to, say what she didn't dare say, and go alone where she would never dream to venture. In return for my audacity, I got praise not just from her but from my father, who never ever looked down on me because I was a girl – why should that stop him from treating me like a son? I was his mouthpiece, too. If I had a brain, it was because I had his brain, and he was determined to make sure I used it properly. One of the first sentences he tried to teach me was, 'God does not exist.' One of my first responses was, 'Yes, John, but . . .'

When we moved to Turkey, my duties as their part-time honorary alter-ego became more varied still. From the age of eight, I was the one who ordered the meals, bargained with the taxi drivers, bought the tickets, and booked the hotels during our long trips through the Middle East and Europe. It wasn't always easy. I was good at picking up languages, but not as good as my father assumed. I remember, two weeks into our first trip to Greece, how he marched me to the door of a windmill in Skiros, where a toothless old lady stood curiously waiting, and said, 'Charm this woman and then ask her for two rooms.' I did not charm her. And I did not get us two rooms. Because I got the Greek word for rooms – *domatia* – slightly wrong: all she would give me was two tomatoes.

Despite my many failures, my father continued to have a rice button approach to foreign languages: he thought that, if I could speak Greek during a game of Red Light, Green Light, then I also had to know the Greek words for all the parts of a car, even the parts I couldn't name in English. I remember listening miserably to his long, staccato explanation about a faulty carburettor, and then turning to the waiting mechanic and saying, 'The car is broken.' Which is not to say I always translated accurately when I did know the words. Asked to tell a lecherous fisherman he had a beautiful singing voice, I said instead, 'My father says he'll kill you if you dare to touch me or my sister.' Asked to tell an unhelpful hotel clerk that he was a son of a bitch, I remember saying, 'My father will be very angry if you phone the police because he has a powerful uncle who works at the Embassy.'

Our hierarchy was uncertain. I was disciplined like a child, protected and coddled and championed like a child, but unless I was being told to set the table or put my shoes where they belonged, I was addressed as an adult. I did not have any real responsibilities, but I was assumed to be, and so thought of myself as being, the person in charge. Not just when we were travelling, but whenever my parents' colourful but harmless bohemian social life turned them temporarily into children. 'Maureen was twenty-one years old the day we were born.' That was one of their favourite sayings. Combine it with one of the other comments I heard a lot at the start of adolescence. 'I never thought I'd see you turn into a teenager but it's finally happened.' Who was speaking – a parent who was worried about losing a child? Or a child who was worried about losing a parent? If the answer was both of the above, then which question did I fear most?

The jury was still out on these questions when Matthew was born. So having a child and becoming a parent was bound to cause some confusion, and this confusion was bound to feed into my struggles to balance home and work. I wanted to be independent and I wanted to be cared for. I wanted to think for myself and I wanted to be protected from my mistakes. I wanted to be a child, and I wanted to be a parent, or rather, both parents. I wanted to be my mother, running a secret society devoted to children, cooking and satire in the kitchen, and I wanted to be my father, keeping whatever hours he wished in his study, emerging only for beautifully cooked meals of which he almost always received the largest serving. I wanted to take turns being the one and then the other, with Paul playing whichever person I didn't happen to want to be at that time. I had a very clear idea about the kind of unconditional support I wanted from my mother when I was being my father, and my father when I was being my mother. I had only the sketchiest ideas about the kind of unconditional support I should be giving in return. I was unwilling, unable even, to cede any control over childcare – I knew in my bones that I knew best – just as I was unwilling and unable to think of myself as a breadwinner – because, just as instinctively, I knew I would fail.

All equal parents are alike. But parents who start out unequal, who come into it unequal to the job, are unequal in different ways. As I launch into my own peculiar tragicomedy, what I would ask you to look at is neither how I made a mess of things, nor how I prevailed against the odds, even though, like most parents, I did both. What I would ask you to look at are the ideas I took with me as I set off for the light at the end of the tunnel, propelled by forces I could neither control nor identify, and aided only by the ideological equivalent of a weak flashlight. I may have given up on the idea that the body was the site of oppression. Kate Millett and *Sexual Politics* notwithstanding, I knew that there was more to men and women than domination and submission. I knew that, contrary to what our great psychiatric thinkers told us, childrearing was more than a mother and a child sitting in a moral and social vacuum. I even knew that, just because a man wanted to be an equal parent, this did not automatically mean that he could become one, or even be allowed to become one. But I still cherished this bizarre and never-examined idea that Paul and I were two machines who were joined at the hip and made up of interchangeable parts. And so I still believed that all we needed to do to change ourselves and therefore the world was to get the combination right.

'I see you're making good use of the baby's naptimes,' my mother said to me with a bright and knowing smile when she came to visit me six months later. And I was. The moment the baby's eyelids drooped, I was offloading him into the cot, and then rushing to my notebook to take up mid-sentence and sometimes mid-word the cramped and frantic notes I was making towards the new novel. That this novel would not happen quickly enough to solve our urgent money problems went without saying. Just as Paul had worked it out in his head that the baby was my problem, so I had worked it out in my head that the money was his problem. I was rushing to the notebook for myself. All I wanted to do at that point was keep my brain exercised. The surge of anger I felt when a cry from the cot forced me to abandon the notebook was not yet too strong to contain or even deny. I still felt right about postponing real work until such a time as I could be sure it did not detract in any conceivable way from my little darling's perfect existence.

Gradually the call of the notebook grew louder and more urgent. His first birthday came and went. As friends began to enter the picture, our schedule grew more complicated. I decided that the only way to find myself working time without making him suffer for it was to join a playgroup with my new friends. The idea was for two mothers to look after five toddlers on a rotating basis once a week for two and a half hours. It was pleasant being able to take my notebook down to North Beach three Fridays out of every five, but it did not take long to figure out that this was a cumbersome and complicated way to get next to nothing written.

Still unwilling to make the baby pay for the releasing of my now almost erotic desire to use my brain, I tried nights. My brain didn't co-operate. Next I tried early mornings, but I would always take longer to wake up than I expected, and Matthew would always wake up just as I was getting going. This would put me in a bad mood for breakfast. Although I was quite sure I had managed to keep my increasingly murderous thoughts from hurting the baby, I convinced myself that it was only a matter of time before the dam burst. The search for the perfect child–work compromise grew more urgent.

I had to get back to my novel, I had to, I had to! But I could not bear the idea of leaving Matthew with a babysitter who might ruin him for life. There was not just safety to think about. There was the problem of separation. Discipline. Nutrition. Gender formation! There was only one person I could trust to do things our way, to say, 'You did something bad, Matthew,' instead of, 'You are a bad boy,' who would feed him from all four food-groups three times a day without overdoing any substance that might be mucus-forming, only one person who could make sure that he did not suffer a drop in standard of care because I happened to be doing something for myself, and that person was Paul. So I approached him. Using, in my nervousness, a nursery-school-teacher voice. I had to get back to work, I explained. Because I could not pretend that this work would bring in any money in the near future, I was willing to put his work schedule first. But his schedule did not seem full to me, I told him! It would be easy to rearrange things so that we could take turns working in the office he had rented in North Beach. One of us could go down to the office at the crack of dawn. The other could go down in the afternoon. We could even all meet for lunch! Paul said no, reminding me that he had a book under contract that was due by the end of the summer.

He advised me to look for a babysitter. I decided to hire a local teenager to come in after school two afternoons a week. The idea was that she would watch *Sesame Street* with Matthew in our bedroom while I worked at our dining-room table. On her first day of work, Matthew cried for an hour and then she dropped him on his head.

It was weeks before I was confident that the damage wasn't permanent. It was months before I resumed the search for a babysitter. By now Paul had gone back to El Paso for a few months, to do research for the novel. Meanwhile, I had been hired quite suddenly to do the treatment for a screenplay. Pressed for time, I hired my first undocumented worker. Odilia was an El Salvadoran refugee who had come to San Francisco to be closer to a Cuban evangelist who operated out of the Mission District. For three months, she took such warm care of Matthew that my guilt about leaving him turned slowly into a benign combination of awe and jealousy.

In the beginning, while Paul was away, I used the large oak desk in his North Beach office. Then, when he got back, he arranged to rent the office next to it for me. The desk I bought for it would not have been large enough for a six year old. But it was the perfect size for my shrunken ego, not to mention my shrunken sense of obligation to bring in money.

For three months, we had what seemed like a perfect routine. Every morning I would take Matthew out to his activities and his friends. We would return home to find Odilia halfway through making a beautiful chicken soup. Paul and I would walk down to North Beach for a Chinese lunch and then go to our offices to work until six. Our first hint that something was amiss was when neighbours reported that Odilia had been receiving a male visitor in our apartment while we were away on a short holiday. But I decided not to confront her with that. My reasoning was that, if I acted the heavy, and she had to leave, it would be Matthew who would suffer. As it turned out, she left anyway.

In lieu of notice, she provided us with a replacement. Eluisa was a grandmother who went to Odilia's church. She did not seem quite equal to the challenge of a toddler, but over the weeks that followed, she was able to exert what seemed to be a magical but not entirely benign calming influence. Matthew's appetite went off. He had a perpetual cold and no energy. On what turned out to be Eluisa's last day, we came home unexpectedly early to find him surrounded by the possible reasons – a plate piled high with ageing éclairs, a bowl of soup that had both mould and bones in it, and an open bottle of children's aspirin.

My confidence in undocumented workers shattered, I opted for a playground run by a single mother with teacher training. This turned out to be illegal, too. Apparently she couldn't apply for permission because the regulations required a ramp for the handicapped. The first day I took Matthew there, he went straight up to the other children, and one by one, knocked them down. I reprimanded him in my usual careful way. The single mother said, 'If you don't mind, I'll let the kids work this out on their own.' When I got back that afternoon, she told me that they had and that she didn't think he was ever going to try 'the pure aggression route again'. Alarmed, I considered never returning. But when I did, he was so eager to join his friends that I could barely take his coat off before he streaked away from me.

Despite this proof that I was not quite as important as I thought I was, and that my careful discipline was ineffectual, I continued to agonise over the damage I might be doing to him by working. When we moved to rural Connecticut not long after his second birthday, I could have put him into full-time daycare, as there was a good Mormon-run nursery not far from where we lived. Instead I opted for three hours every morning, so that I would have time to socialise with him in the afternoons.

As it turned out, no friends or playmates materialised. Although it soon became clear that Matthew would have had more fun in daycare, and although our bank account desperately needed the money that I might be able to make if I ever finished my novel, I clung to our unsatisfactory schedule. It was partly because I was afraid of working longer hours, because I knew that if I did I would finish my novel sooner, and so find out sooner and in a public and humiliating way that it wasn't worth anything. It wasn't until the September before he was four, when we moved back to El Paso, that I dared to enrol him in a Montessori school for a wicked six hours a day. I did this because by now I was pregnant again, and I was desperate to finish my long-suffering novel before the new baby arrived that May.

And I did finish it, this despite the fact that I had to spend the last ten weeks in bed, first with flu, then with pneumonia, and then under anxiety-producing medicine that managed to keep my persistent cough from sending me into labour before the due date. It was work, I think, that helped keep my mind off my worries. Although I had every reason to be apprehensive. After I had gone through nine hours of foetal distress, my doctor decided that a marginal placenta praevia was blocking the cervix. She decided for an emergency Caesarean, but this was easier said than done, because it was the first sunny Sunday of the spring. She was at the bottom of her surgeon list before she could find one with his bleeper working. She couldn't find an anaesthetist for the same reason. But they had both turned up by the time they had fixed the lift I got stuck in on my way to the operating room.

To the surprise of the doctors who had mismanaged my labour, the baby was born healthy. When I took her home, the first thing I did was turn my desk into a changing table. I had finished my novel, I had won a grant, and I wanted to spend a year or two enjoying this last baby before twisting myself out of shape again. What was the rush? This time I knew what lay ahead, or at least I thought I did.

Then, when the baby was five months old, the editor who bought my novel did so only on condition that I rewrote the middle third. I hired our nice Mexican cleaner to do six hours a week of babysitting. The revisions were failing to progress nicely when, three months later, Paul and I decided that we had to change our lives again, and fast, or get stuck in Texas for ever. He didn't want to spend the rest of his life teaching creative writing. He wanted to go back to university for another degree. Because I wanted to go back to England, I talked him into applying to Oxford. There remained the problem of his unfinished novel. If he was going to go back to school, we both agreed, he shouldn't have this hanging over his head. The best thing, we decided, was for him to go to Mexico to

finish it, while I stayed in El Paso and finished his teaching
contract.

II

Now, suddenly, for the first time in my life, and without having
had the time to reflect on the implications, I was working for
money. The vague and menacing questions about right and
wrong reasons, good and bad care, the perfect home-and-work
balance, faded away under the glare of practicalities. Here I was,
alone in a condominium complex with a four year old and an
eight-month-old baby who had to be rocked for an hour before
she went to sleep and still woke up between five and eight times
a night. Now, in addition to my revisions, I had to take on this
job for which I had no experience. How the hell was I going
to do it?

The solution was complicated. It involved two babysitters.
One was a legal but somewhat charmless local teenager. The
other was the warm, and vastly entertaining, but illegal Delia.
Her cooking and her way with the children made it more
than worth my while to do ten trips a week to the Mexican
border. As we drove back and forth, back and forth, along
the same desolate stretch of the Rio Grande, she rewarded
me with the latest episodes from the soap opera she said
was her life. It involved a treacherous husband with lipstick
on his collar, a former suitor turned traffic policeman named
Lorenzo, a savagely beaten daughter, and a revenge involving
a *mariachi* band.

I had one other friend in El Paso. We met through the
children's school. Because it was a drive-in nursery, at first I
only knew (and disdained) her as the driver of a Mercedes Benz
with California plates. We made friends almost accidentally at
a birthday party. She was Greek, from Samos. She had once
been a sociology professor, but had not managed to find a
new post when her husband, a physicist, also a Greek, moved
them from New York to California. So she had retrained to
become a lawyer. She had managed to finish on schedule
despite giving birth to a daughter not long before her finals.
Babysitter problems had foiled her first attempt at passing

the California bar, but after her second, successful, attempt, she quickly found the ideal job with a woman state supreme court justice. She was just finding her feet when her husband decided to retrain to become a doctor and enrolled himself in an accelerated course on the other side of the Rio Grande at Juarez Medical School. My friend Zoë and her daughter Amalia followed. As the California bar was not recognised in Texas, Zoë was forced to enrol in yet another bar-review course.

By the time it began, her husband was through with Juarez and doing his first year of residency in Chicago. His plan was to return to Texas for the second and subsequent years. Because her childcare crisis coincided with my childcare crisis, we pooled our resources, and helped each other out not just with driving and babysitters and meals but with weekends. We divided our Saturdays and Sundays up so that we each got four hours of working time a day. On Saturday nights we went out with all the children to a Tex-Mex bar where we had nachos, cheeseburgers, and margaritas. We took turns driving and overindulging.

We got used to the technical difficulties and started to relax. After a terrifying start, I found I liked teaching. My revisions started to write themselves. I lost weight, gained confidence. Zoë got a job with the most interesting law firm in the city. There was a promotion and a rise awaiting her as soon as she had passed the bar. But then, as she was getting ready to sit the last day of the exam, her husband rang from Chicago to tell her that he had changed his mind, and that he would be finishing his residency in Chicago. The State of Illinois does not recognise either the California or the Texas bar. Now she faced another two-year hiatus, another bar-review course, another exam, another round of job hunting without connections.

That Saturday, when we went out for our margaritas, Zoë was very gloomy. To cheer her up, I suggested that her new business card should read, 'Zoë Petrides, if you want me, I'm at the bar.' But she didn't laugh. It turned out to be our last women-only outing, because the next day Paul came back unexpectedly early from Mexico with the news that he had been accepted on a postgraduate course at Oxford.

III

Matthew was old enough to start school when we got to England, but Emma was still only a toddler. Our financial masterplan depended on my finishing a novel in a year, but I didn't want Emma to go without friends just because I was working. So as soon as we were settled, I went into a nanny-share. This turned out to be complicated, and not just because I collapsed in the middle of the year with pneumonia. One of the mothers was French and hated the English because they put ugly clothes on their children and didn't heat their houses. Another was English and hated the French because they spent too much money on children's clothes and kept their houses too hot. One was high up in the Conservative Party and hated scruffiness. Another cultivated dirty fingernails and canvassed for Labour. It was hard to keep the peace, all the more so when the nanny began to suffer almost biweekly tragedies that prevented her from coming into work. If she herself hadn't suffered from a concussion, it was her roommate who had come down with a mysterious African disease while cycling on the Isle of Man. If it wasn't a brother who had wrapped himself and his car around a tree, it was an aunt or a cousin. It took me a year to tell her that I didn't believe her, and when I did, I shouted at her in a voice so ugly it scared me as much as it did her. I never saw her again.

By now I was only on speaking terms with two of the other mothers. We were done with nannies, but we could not find suitable nurseries that would have us. So we helped set up a co-operative playgroup. This worked out well for the children, not so well for us because some of the partners were more co-operative than others. I was a substitute. In the first half of the year, I ended up doing more work at the playgroup than I did at my desk. In the second half of the year, the two other mothers argued and then split into rival playgroups. I sent Emma to both of them. I also got pneumonia a few more times.

I did not finish the novel.

The day arrived when we had nothing to live on, and no work papers either. Paul and I decided to write a quick commercial novel together. He wrote the first draft, and I wrote the second. By the time it became apparent that no one was going to buy it, we had run through our credit. Paul flew off to Chicago to make some quick money working for an old schoolfriend. I stayed in England with the children, took out Irish citizenship and got myself reviewing work. This had always been my idea of hell, to write for a large audience without having time to get things right, and to have to live with your mistakes for ever after. It seemed particularly hellish to me at the time, because I had not been able to finish even a sentence for going on two years. Halfway through my first review, my typewriter broke. My French friend was kind enough to lend me hers. It wasn't until I had sat down to type a sentence of gobbledegook that I discovered her typewriter had a French keyboard. But I felt I had no choice but to persist. To my surprise, I found out that I could get things done, even if I had the wrong typewriter, if I had an immovable deadline.

IV

Money continued to be scarce. Things did improve after Paul got his work papers. But the jobs were demoralising. First there was a property magazine, which he wrote cover to cover – very depressing if your salary doesn't even cover the rent. Then he edited a commercial newsletter and a bodybuilding magazine – until he ran an article criticising steroids. I brought some money in with reviewing work. After I found a childminder for Emma in the afternoons, I also took up translating. But my novel would not get off the ground. And my health was poor. I kept coming down with pneumonia. I developed a cyst in my breast and had to be operated on.

Paul and I had always argued. Now we did nothing but argue. So when Paul was offered a job teaching in Miami, he talked them into letting us split it and take it in turns. This seemed the best solution as neither of us wanted to move the family to Miami and then regret it. We also hoped that the temporary separation would give us both time to think. I went over by myself to do the first semester, leaving Paul and my parents to look after the children. My hope was that I would be able to use the four months alone to finish the novel that was now dragging into its fourth unsuccessful year. In the end, I used the four months alone to stare at the ceiling and order unusual meals from restaurants that made home deliveries. It took two pay-cheques for the facts of economic life to become starkly apparent. I could not support myself in one country, and Paul and the children in the other, on one modest salary.

The same fact had made itself clear to Paul. He began to look for work. Just before Christmas, he rang me to say that he had found himself a job in London. I flew back to England to decide whether we had a future together. When the answer turned out to be no, we packed up the house. On New Year's Day, he moved to London and the children and I flew to Miami to finish the contract. I gave Matthew and Emma the bedroom of my student housing efficiency unit and set up a camp bed for myself in the kitchen.

I spent the next week trying to find the doctors who would give them the injections and TB tests without which no school would admit them. Then came the challenge of smuggling Matthew, now eight, into a district where primary schools were said to be free of handguns. By the time I had solved that, and attended the obligatory parental training seminars at Emma's gestapo-run nursery school, both children were suspended because they had nits in their hair. The nits were dead, but dead was not good enough for the State of Florida. The children were not readmitted to school until I had removed every single nit. By the time I had done so, I had come down with pneumonia. No sooner was I back on my feet, than my car broke down. Then Matthew got strep throat. Then I only barely succeeded in keeping Emma from being suspended from school again. My crime this time was to have failed to produce a specific kind of home-made cookie for a bake sale, even though I had signed a contract that bound me to do so. My excuse was that my efficiency unit didn't have an oven. They said this wasn't good enough. It was only at the last minute that they relented and said I could provide them with thirty-five baggies of trail mix.

Then my car broke down again. Then the children started waking up with nightmares. It turned out the babysitter I was using was letting them watch things like *Nightmare on Elm Street*. I stopped using babysitters. If I had to go to a poetry reading, or a work-related dinner, I took the children with me. But I was too distraught to do so thoughtfully. Once, when we were on our way to fetch an unusually picky poet, and Emma was shrieking in the back seat, I told her that, if she didn't pipe down, I would hire a new babysitter called Vampira. She reported me the next day to her nursery school teacher. I got a reprimand.

Then Matthew got nits again. Once again, he was barred from school until such a time as a doctor could provide a clean bill of hair. It took me a day to find a doctor who would give us an appointment. It was nine at night by the time we had the prescription. At ten o'clock, the pharmacist was just handing me the desired package when the store was closed down, with the prescription still in it, due to a bomb scare. I threw a tantrum outside the store, hoping they would let me into the store again after the all-clear. When they told me that they were just going to close the store for the night, the tantrum turned into full-blown hysteria. They sent me home. I was on my way to pick up the prescription the next morning when my car broke down again.

I was not in good shape by now. Work had become something you got through. My novel was stuck on page 58. I could pull myself together to teach, I could even enjoy it, but the moment the bell rang ending class, the screaming in my head returned, and with it the free-floating anxiety and the unreasonable tears. I was not a good mother. I had no patience. I screamed at them, I screamed in front of them. The only time I could cope with them was when we were out. We spent the weekends trailing aimlessly from beach to pool to restaurant to unsuitable movie. I would look at them after they were asleep and say to myself: I'm thirty-five and I can't even give my kids a home. It was only after we got back to England that I found out they had liked Miami, and even missed it, because 'it was the only time we ever did things together'.

V

I had originally intended to spend the summer in England and then return to Miami with the children in the autumn, as my contract had been renewed. Paul wanted us to stay in England, in accordance with our separation agreement, but as I didn't have a job in England, I thought it might be a good idea to hold on to the one that I did have in Miami. While I was prevaricating, Paul became convinced that I might try and smuggle the children out of the country, and so he took the children's passports. I was told that he was within his rights to do so and also that I was unlikely to get permission to take the children out of the country without his consent. Although I knew I would have taken the passports, too, if I had been in his shoes, and even though I half admired him for doing what he had to do to keep his children close to him, there was still part of me that felt tricked and trapped.

Now it was not a question of balancing the demands of children with the demands of work, but a question of choosing between them. Without pausing to think, I chose the children, chose also to stay in Oxford, where I hoped their old school and old friends would see them through the divorce. I prided myself on having faced the truth about my inadequacies as a parent, and having arranged for them to get the bare basics from people with better track records. I returned to my never-finishing novel, but only during schooltime, and weekends when the children were with Paul – anything more would have been sacrilege. The rest of my time I devoted to sulking.

I steeled myself for a life alone. From now on, I would define my identity through work. Then I met Frank, who was as unhappy as I was and for much the same reasons. Like me, Frank had come here intending to stay a year or two. Then he had married an Englishwoman who had initially promised to go back to the US with him, then changed her mind after failing to be impressed by the country during their honeymoon visit. Now they had two children. He was, like me, anchored in England. Unlike me, he was still married.

This didn't stop me falling in love with him. At first it was nothing but pleasure. The trouble began one Sunday morning when he rang me while he was cooking his family a big breakfast, and I wanted to be there.

The more I tried to talk myself out of it, the stronger the desire became. For no good reason, but probably for the reason I was happy to see him do all the things that had aggravated me so much when Paul did them, like leaving his shoes in front of the television, I wanted to be there. As time wore on, the desire became more involved. Soon I wanted to be there not just with Frank, but with his children and my children. To this fantasy I eventually added *our* children.

Wicked! I deserved to be locked up. And so I asked for nothing, and hoped that one day the dream might come true without my doing anything wilful or selfish. Eighteen months passed. The rituals of contact ceased to hold. One short telephone conversation a day turned gradually into a one- or two-hour conversation every morning, afternoon, and evening. Methods of subterfuge went from prudent to daring to farcical. Work suffered. Which is not to say I stopped trying, just that it took longer than ever to get things done, harder to tear myself away from it. There was one evening when I lost track of the time while trying to finish a book review. It was eleven o'clock when the children asked me about supper. All I had in the house, I discovered, was vanilla ice-cream and a packet of stale scones.

It was hard to think about my house, because I spent so much time hearing about *his* house. There I was at the wrong end of the phone unseen, unable to see, but hearing everything: I was there in spirit, all right. I was their household ghost. As I struggled to keep my real life and my ghost life separate, moving now into my fifth year of insomnia, I noticed with a combination of alarm and professional interest that the effort made me feel like two people in the same way that balancing home and work made me feel like two people.

A day came when the obvious presented itself to me in the

form of an inspirational vision. Actually I was not two people, but one person doing a collection of incompatible things. As soon as I became comfortable with this new idea, I began to see that the things I did that made me feel most guilty were precisely the things that allowed others to take advantage of me. Fired up with the anger that followed from this insight, I decided that I wasn't going to sneak around any more. The affair came out in the open and then ended badly. The facts his angry wife threw at me over the phone were too much to take. My landlady happened to drop by that morning and saw the danger signs, so she swept the children off, and marched me up to bed with only just enough sedatives. When I got out of bed three days later, and went downstairs with a pen and a notebook, it was not to find the perfect balance between home and work, or to write my way to freedom, or even to find myself, but to keep my mind busy so that I could stop myself from jumping into a car and driving into an attractive wall at the entrance of Kingston Bagpuize.

The thing I wrote that day was a try-out piece for that newspaper column. It was about the dangers call-waiting posed to adulterers. When I got the column, I despaired of ever finding time to finish my hopeless novel, but over the next year, it resuscitated itself. It, too, was about adultery, a subject that had been a theoretical mystery to me when I had started it seven years earlier. I was doing the finishing touches when Frank came back.

This time, we vowed to each other, we were going to do it right. Five years later we are still trying. If I say we're mostly succeeding, it is with the humbling knowledge that there is no such thing as a new life. Whatever you do, wherever you settle, however you change your ideas, no matter how wise and strong you become, you still take your ghosts with you. And they still lead you blindfolded back to the same old stories.

Until the day comes when the blindfold falls off and you see that despite your best efforts you have passed your ghosts on to your children. And you remember the day when your mother had to face the same horror.

Guiltfest

One of the benefits of having too many children while also working too hard is that you rarely have time to step out of your life and reflect on it. One of the drawbacks of such an existence is that, when circumstances contrive to stop the treadmill, and you do have time to reflect on things, the truth doesn't just come to you. It slaps you in the face. This is what happened to me not long ago when a train I was taking came to an unscheduled stop between two stations.

I had been away on business, but I had stayed longer than I had needed to in order to have lunch with a friend. I had set out for this lunch in a self-righteous mood: it had been months since I had seen this friend, weeks since I had done anything, anything, for myself. It was dangerous if I never did anything for myself. Dangerous for everybody. If I didn't ever do anything selfish, for no other purpose than pleasure, then the day would come when there would be nothing left of me, and if that happened, everyone who depended on me would suffer. My high moral purpose meant that the lunch was intense and significant rather than relaxing. Knowing my friend (who has no children) thought I put far too much time into my family, I took advantage of her indulgent bias to badmouth everybody. So when I realised I had stayed too long, and jumped to my feet, my friend was quick to say, 'Stop feeling so sorry for him. So what, if he has to look after the children for a change?' I told her that I hoped she didn't think that he never looked after the children, because of course he did. Her parting words were, 'Bollocks.'

Had the train kept moving, I would only have been two hours late, but now it was going to be three hours or more. After the guard made his announcement, I had an idea to ring home and tell them what had happened. But while I was looking for my phonecard, I found my car keys instead. The only set of car keys, for the only car that was in working order.

The friend I had had lunch with had just got her decree nisi and had spent the afternoon rejoicing over her new freedom. She had said that she didn't think she ever wanted to share a house with another man again. She told me that she had read

149

in a book by a psychiatrist called Adam Phillips that the main reason why people sought out long-lasting relationships was that relationships stopped them thinking. It now occurred to me that, if that were so, then the opposite of a long-lasting relationship had to be an Intercity 125.

The thoughts that came to me as I stared at the orange seat in front of me! First I remembered all the unkind things I had said over lunch. Then I remembered all the things that were not in her refrigerator. Then I conjured up the children's faces as they waited outside their schools for the car that had never arrived. How had Frank got home from work? Who had collected the children or were they still standing there? Had the nanny had to walk to the local shops to buy food for lunch? Where were they all now? Were they angry with me? Weren't they right to be? Why hadn't I found the keys sooner? Why had I taken them in the first place? What did this mistake say about me, my true agenda, my unconscious? Why had I not gone home when I should have done? The more I thought, the more virulent my regrets became. By the time the train started moving again, I had been visited by every mistake I had made during my marriage, every miscalculation that had damaged my children for life, every misconceived dream that had contributed to the mess I was in now. It was my fault that we had more bills than money and more children than bedrooms or seats in the car. My fault that, in order to make up the difference, I had become a harder and more aggressive person than I had ever wanted to be. It was my fault that Frank's children and my older children had had to suffer through two divorces, and for what? I remembered the grand statements I had made at the time, about dignity and peace of mind and finding a better way. And I remembered the visions of happiness that had sustained me. Could I have been serious? In addition to breaking up two homes for a house of dreams, in addition to lying about these dreams to the people around me, for years and years and years I had also been lying to myself.

And lying especially about my motives. I liked to think of myself as a martyr who had to work too hard for the noblest of reasons. But whose idea had this family been in the first place? By the time we got to Bath I had seen the monstrous truth: the only time I could feel any pleasure at any work well done was when I could convince myself that my family would have starved or gone homeless without it. It was true, I had created a family to hide inside so that I could satisfy my ambitions without ever having to face my feelings.

In so doing, I had failed my children utterly. I had failed them by making them too much like me. I had failed them also by trying so many stupid ideas out on them. Whatever they went on to do, whatever mistakes they made in life, it would be partly because of what I had so thoughtlessly imposed on them, and blindly passed on to them. They were my creations: and so they were my fault. But just as horrifying were the things I had not created, and not been able to change. I thought about the world I was about to throw them into. Which was worse than it ever was, because people like me had not managed to make any difference at all, because we had become so caught in the minutiae of balancing home and work that the only time we ever stepped out of our lives and reflected on them was when we happened to find ourselves on a stretch of track that was experiencing signal failure.

It was all my fault, all my fault, everything. The fact that everyone else had made the same mistakes was hardly a consolation. We had all failed, and so we were all doomed. And so were our children. And that was when I thought I knew how my mother had felt all those years ago when she saw me, her own faulty creation, set out to fulfil her secret ambitions in a world that had no room for them. She had felt like Frankenstein, looking at his monster. And now so did I.

Then I got home, to find Rachel wearing a tiger mask, staring out the window, flapping her arms. Supper was on the stove. The nanny looked cheerful, which meant there had been no mishaps in my absence. Frank was sitting at the kitchen table doing a crossword puzzle, while Pandora walked around and around the kitchen table wearing his shoes. She paused every few feet to take a drink from her bottle. Kimber was in the far corner, building her a Duplo tower, and Emma was sitting next to him reading a teen magazine, while also arguing with him about the Whale and Dolphin Conservation Society.

Helen, the three year old, was standing on a chair watching

the goldfish fly. Matthew had taken the lid off the tank to show her that they weren't flying but swimming. She dipped her hand into the water, then looked up and asked him if fish fingers swam too.

As I listened to him explain why they didn't, I started looking at the fish tank through her eyes. For a split second I could see fish fingers mingling peacefully with the goldfish. Turning from the impossible to the child who had imagined it, I remembered why she was here and why I was here and how much I liked it here, and how sorry I would be when the children grew up and left. I closed my eyes and looked at my guilty thoughts, looked at them from the outside instead of swimming in circles inside them, and came to the following conclusions:

7

THE PATRIARCHY – AN UPDATE

Another look at guilt

'Guilt, guilt, guilt,' Ros Coward fumes in *Our Treacherous Hearts*:[1]

> At one point I felt as though I would never hear about anything else. One after another, women claimed they had 'the monopoly on guilt' or they had 'invented it'. One woman told me that she felt guilty that her first husband had left her – she must have neglected the relationship. Many told me they felt guilty for not having sex often enough with their partners. Equal numbers told me they felt guilty about their mothers or sisters, especially if they felt their own material circumstances and opportunities were better than those of other members of their family. There was guilt from women who had loved their childminders more than their mothers, guilt from women who felt they loved their mothers too much, to the detriment of their relationships with their husbands. Overwhelmingly there was guilt at not doing things well enough – '*anything* well enough', said one woman, speaking from the ranks of ordinary women who neither receive satisfaction from their work nor feel that they are being particularly effective in the home.

Ros Coward interprets this as a sign 'that women are internalising the conflicts of their current position rather than finding social solutions'.[2] Going on to quote Melanie Klein, who said that 'ambivalence breeds guilt and guilt in its turn fosters masochistic submission', she says that this goes some way towards explaining why women comply with traditional sexual division:

> Guilt seems to accompany any attempt to break with tradi-
> tional structures, and indeed any *thought* of breaking that
> structure. And ambivalence does seem to be central here.
> When there are two strong impulses in play – such as the
> desire to follow a career and the belief that a child benefits
> from its mother's attention – then the feelings of guilt are
> particularly intense.[3]

She concludes that, while the fears surrounding the real responsibilities of mothering are to be respected, there still seems to be room for the Kleinian argument that:

> The unconscious compulsion behind excessive guilt from a
> mother to her own child [might be] an obsessive fear that her
> baby might feel the retaliatory rage towards her that she once
> felt towards her own mother. No wonder a mother suffers
> such anxiety and guilt. Any amount of sacrifice is worth it
> to avoid such hostile, destructive feelings. What professional
> achievements could justify such a risk?[4]

It is because we are afraid to own up to the treacheries in our own hearts, she says, that our courage has failed us. It's because we've been deeply dishonest about our motives at home and at work that our dreams haven't come true.

Yes, well, perhaps. But the time has come to take a hard look at the patriarchal nightmare that our presumed failure of courage has allowed to prevail instead. The subtitle for *Our Treacherous Hearts* is *Why We Let Men Have Their Way.* The Gothic romance this suggests is all about a generation of women who once had standards, revolutionary clarity, and fighting spirit but then lost their nerve when they found it too difficult to balance work and home. Exhausted by the logistics, unwilling to acknowledge the tumultuous and conflicting feelings that motherhood produced in them, but all too willing to win the approval of the men in their lives by being weak, passive, and childish, these women allowed themselves to fall back into their traditional roles, where convention permitted and even encouraged them to shun self-awareness, and where collective action was impossible.

Ros describes her own journey into this rut: the retreat from the:

> . . . confident Utopian feminism of my twenties to a conventional family structure and a lack of any organised feminist politics in my thirties. When pregnant with my first child, I never dreamt that I would contemplate giving up work, let alone be happy to. Yet when it came to a choice between a daily motorway drive to a job which did not fire my enthusiasm, and a small child to look after at home, the decision was easy. I gave up my university job and went freelance, cutting my hours of work, thereby pushing my partner and myself into a division of labour that neither of us had ever anticipated. Once that decision had been taken, virtually every woman I met seemed to tell a similar story. I could no longer avoid the question of how much women themselves collude in keeping the conventional structures in place.[5]

And she's right, up to a point. Every working mother has given in to outside pressures, instead of 'holding out' for social and economic change. Whenever I give in myself, I feel the same way Ros does, that I'm proving unworthy of my feminist dreams and letting men have their way.

When I say men in this mood, I mean all men, as well as all the cultural conventions, laws and institutions that help them keep the upper hand. I mean the men who run the country, the men I work for, the men who decide on the size of my overdraft, control my children's schooling, and refuse to allow working parents' needs on to the political agenda. When I say men in this mood, the ones who lack faces have a way of merging with the ones who have faces. Their invisible power gives resonance to every foible and transgression I can trace to a man with a face. If the man who's lying next to me in bed feigns sleep when the baby wakes up in the middle of the night, he quickly ceases to be a man who's trying to shirk a duty I would prefer to shirk myself, and reveals himself to be a wicked patriarch. If, despite this moment of truth, I end up going back to bed with him, if I still crave the warmth of his body in spite of having identified him as the enemy, it must mean I'm in sexual thrall to him, and as much a slave to pleasure as the frivolous mothers Mary Wollstonecraft so detested.

Ninety-nine point nine nine nine per cent of feminist texts I've ever read are suffused with the fear of succumbing to female desires. Although they define female desires in many different ways, they almost invariably define one type of desire as dangerous. If it's not the desire for sexual pleasure that brings women down, it's the desire for children. If it's not the desire for children, it's the desire for men. Rarely is the idea entertained that it might be possible to live a full life while entertaining and acting on desires for men, children *and* sex. Underpinning even the most ambitious Utopian dreams is this paradoxical assumption that, in order to have a full life, you have to make sure you never desire at least one of the above.

And so these feminist texts are suffused with guilt about the desire for men, or for sex, or for children. Are guiltily aware of the political consequences of succumbing to these desires. Are attempts to provide an escape from this fear and that guilt. Mary Wollstonecraft hoped that education would save women from themselves. The suffragettes hoped it would be the vote. Simone de Beauvoir thought it was living outside motherhood and marriage. Betty Friedan said it was finding a job outside the house. Germaine Greer thought it was by redesigning your sexual identity. Dorothy Dinnerstein, who called the problem the 'malaise about our sexual arrangements', thought it was equal parenting that would make the uncomfortable comfortable again. Kate Millett and Adrienne Rich thought it was the separate peace of political lesbianism.

Where the guilt and the fear and the desire for sex and men and children persist anyway, and when they inform the choices of ordinary and extraordinary women, feminists are quick to interpret this to mean that the conspiracy of patriarchs has scored another victory, and scored it by playing on a woman's sexual weaknesses, by giving her sexual approval only when she acts against her own interests, by making her so desperate for pleasure and approval and traditional support that she is willing to surrender all her higher aims in order to get them.

This is a compelling fairy-tale, but a fairy-tale none the less. And like all fairy-tales, it is made of wishes and fears and inversions. All of which are significant, all of which suggest interesting theories about the aspects of pleasure and sex and children and femininity that feminists find difficult to manage. But we are not looking at facts when we look at this fairy-tale. Where facts exist at all, they exist in a distorted form and/or out of context. Facts that do not fit into the story get shunted aside as inconsequential or atypical. Their exclusion only makes the story more convincing. As Hemingway said, fiction depends more on what it leaves out than what it leaves in.

What this feminist myth leaves out is the idea that the desire for pleasure and love and procreation might be problematic, in different ways, to both sexes. And that such desires cannot help but be problematic in any society where sex and fertility are regulated by rules. Which, as far as I can tell, means any society. By promising us that feminism offers an escape from the problems of desire – for men, love, pleasure, *and* children – and by suggesting that we have only achieved equality to the degree that we are free from the tyranny of these desires, our great feminist thinkers are offering us the impossible and setting us up for a fall. In so doing, they are not just making us feel ashamed of being human, but also making us blind to what it *is* to be human.

Just for argument's sake, let's take apart the myth behind the Ros Coward story, which is the myth behind just about any modern feminist text, and let's consider it piece by piece. Just how accurately does it reflect your experience? To what degree have you really let men have their way? I mean, really? Have they won every last round? Isn't there anything you do together *but* compete? Is there any room for joint ventures? Any middle ground between pure and perfect total resistance and going ooh, ahh, have me any way you like, darling, and opening your legs?

When you leave work for home, do you turn your brain off the moment you walk through the door? When you close the door on the outside world (how long for? A lifetime? A year? A long weekend?) are the women you've met through your children *all* bovine miseries? Aren't you at all proud of your children? Or do you sincerely believe that you have, in your subjugated blindness, created yet another generation of gender robots?

Haven't you ever asked yourself why so few theories about parents, children, and families reflect even a passing familiarity with your everyday life?

A few everyday vignettes

Matthew comes home from school complaining about a teacher who ordered him to put his uniform jacket on and then shouted at him, rudely, when he did not comply at once. 'What a geek,' he says. 'He's never done a thing to earn my respect, and now he expects me to obey him. I felt like hitting him, but don't worry, Mum, I punched the wall instead.' He shows me his fist. Aghast at the bloody spectacle, I warn him he is going to have a hard time in life unless he learns how to hide his feelings. 'You can't expect the real world to operate according to the same rules as this household. If that teacher heard you, you're going to be in terrible trouble,' I say. And he says, 'Don't worry, Mum. I muffled the expletive.'

The phone rings. It's my sister, to tell me about my niece, who had the privilege, unheard of in our day, of being an altar girl when a cardinal from Rome went to say Mass at her parish church. Her job was to pass him the cloth to clean the chalice before communion. When she handed him the wrong one – a wrinkled, dusty rag – he gave it right back and indicated the proper cloth with his forefinger. Her response was to roll her eyes and make a face. Then she beckoned to her mother, pointed at the cardinal, and mouthed the words, 'Can you believe this guy? What a fusspot!'

'The cardinal's little pink hat was shaking with fury,' my sister tells me. 'Everyone was staring at me. I was mortified, but as you know, this isn't new. The liberties I let her take with me, she takes with everyone else. I have created a monster.'

*   *   *

What power, to create a monster. What a shock, when it disappears the moment you set foot outside the house. A few years ago, when I was swimming to recover from an operation and the pneumonia that had succeeded it, a lifeguard told me to get out of the swimming pool because he didn't like the way I had left my children watching me on the side. 'But they know how to swim!' I protested. 'I'm just playing it safe by keeping them there. This is not just for pleasure. I'm doing it for my health.' I told him about the operation, and he said, 'Now that you're a mother, your job is not to look after your health but to look after your children.'

I'm sitting on the underground, on my way to meet my friend Ellen for lunch. A woman gets on the train. She looks familiar. It turns out that she is a sub at the paper where I used to work. She had a baby at the same time I had the baby that brought my time there to an end. Like me, she would have liked to have taken real maternity leave, but she was forced to go straight back to work. Her husband had just been made redundant. Another problem: no childcare. Her solution was to sneak the baby into the office in a discreet basket. She used to feed him in the bathroom. The other women kept quiet about it. The men didn't catch on for weeks. When they did notice, they didn't know what to say, but they didn't object, either. How could they? If they hadn't noticed the baby, that meant that the baby wasn't getting in the way. It could never have lasted, but it ended before the baby became mobile because another woman at the paper had a stillbirth. The managing editor decided the baby had to go at that point because he was worried that the sight of it might be too much for this other woman to bear.

How is the baby now? I ask. Wonderful, she says. What are her plans? She tells me she wants to get out of subbing and into writing, but that the money problem is worse than ever: they have had to give up their house and have moved out to the suburbs to live with her mother.

I say goodbye, get off the train, and meet up with my friend Ellen and two of her workmates. Ellen is agitated because her boss just took her to task for taking on weekend work for another part of the company. The reason she agreed to it was the family overdraft, which is large and getting larger. Even though, like most women forced to return to work after over-short maternity leaves, she regrets and resents the loss of time with her children. So she had not taken it well when her boss, who has no children of his own, told her that she was wrong to take this extra assignment as it conflicted with her domestic responsibilities. Her duty was to spend her weekends with her children, he told her. 'I'm so furious I can hardly speak to him. I may never forgive him.'

One of the friends she has brought with her tries to lighten things up by talking about her two-year-old son, whom she is bringing up alone. At breakfast that morning, he had asked her what colour a symphony was. She has a longer commute now that the company has relocated: she insists it is a blessing in disguise because it gives her more time to read. The problem is that she has to leave the office at six to get back to the childminder in time, and the men in the office seem to think that is letting the side down. While the childminder probably thinks she's leaving it too late. You can't seem to work without being caught in this bind, she says.

The other woman agrees: she is in a bad mood because she has had to lie, and invent a chiropractor appointment, in order to take her five-year-old daughter to the dentist. She's sick of pretending that she doesn't have children. She's sick of her male colleagues disapproving of her when she does admit it. She feels caught between two worlds and fits into neither. The stay-at-home mothers in her neighbourhood won't come near her either: they disapprove of the hours she keeps. On the rare occasion they deign to cross the picket line, she's afraid to mention anything about work. 'If they found out how high-powered I was, I'd scare them off.' She says she's disillusioned about the women's movement. The last time she went to a women's studies conference, not only did they fail to provide a crèche, they behaved as though she had lost her mind when she asked for one.

I pick up a letter from Frank's sister. It's an aggressively cheerful report on her new job and her third pregnancy. Both are going brilliantly. She's a lawyer. She works in an office with seven other women, and one man, the boss. 'At first he didn't know what to do about us. He couldn't follow the conversations. We'd whip back between affidavits and recipes and childcare problems and political fund-raising drives and he just couldn't follow us. But don't worry. We're civilizing him.'

My old friend Ally rings from California. She tells me that no one will hire her sons as babysitters. 'It's generally accepted that if they're boys they're potential child abusers.'

Waiting to go into my daughter Helen's ballet open day, I run into her best friend Sam's mother. She's in a bad way because her husband keeps changing his mind about her and his mistress. 'What did you and I do wrong?' she asks. 'Why can't we control our men?' This makes me uncomfortable, as I'm not quite sure what she's referring to, or who told her, as I myself have never confided in her. Who has been gossiping about my private life? It must be the cleaner. This makes sense as I found the cleaner through her, and it's the cleaner who has been keeping me posted about the procession of scandals in her household. 'I don't think we did anything wrong,' I say. 'I think we can blame it all on them.' She says, 'Why are men *like* that? What do they want? They never change, do they?'

Then we go in to watch the class of three year olds perform elementary ballet. Four out of the eighteen children are boys. More than half of the parents watching are men. Afterwards, in the cloakroom, Helen and her friend Sam have an argument about whose father has the largest 'peanut'.

I open a letter from an Oxford friend who is now living in Washington. She hasn't been too happy there because all the women in her neighbourhood work full time and leave their children with undocumented workers who don't speak English. She liked it much better in Moscow, her husband's previous posting, because there were quite a few 'intelligent women who actually enjoyed taking care of their own children'.

I haven't spoken to her since August, when she rang to tell me that she was going to take her son out of school and teach him at home. I said that was fine so long as she realised she wasn't just doing it for him, but for herself, because if he started full-time schooling, she would run out of reasons not to work. I regretted being so sharp, and for months I have been phrasing, but, typically, never getting around to committing to paper, a letter of apology. As I open the letter, I think: Well, maybe she's forgiven me. After all, she is a very forgiving person. I open up the letter. A business card falls out. It reads:

Naomi Hartman Ellis
SPOUSE

Emma, once the star of her school football team, and veteran of countless fist fights, but now feeling exotic in an apron, is playing waitress to an empty table. Smiling at the faces only she sees above the carefully arranged plates, she nods as she takes down the inaudible orders, and then moves on to the next customer with a polite, almost amused raised eyebrow and puckered lips.

This game has been going on too long. The first time was when she was four, playing with her first Barbie doll, humming the wedding march, which was only appropriate as the doll had come dressed in a wedding gown. It was a gift from my soon-to-be-ex mother-in-law. She must have rushed out to get it the moment she heard about the impending divorce. 'Who is Barbie marrying?' I remember asking. It was with utter contempt that she told me the obvious: 'The invisible man.'

Matthew is doing the dishes while listening to heavy metal. His hair is in his eyes. When a plate doesn't do as he thinks it ought, he hisses a swear word. Helen is on her toy motor bike. Pandora, quacking like a duck, pushes her off. Emma says, 'Oh Pandora, you're so boyish.' Matthew says, 'Emma, you mustn't say things like that.' Emma says, 'Things like what, you idiot?'

'You mustn't attribute a personality trait to a particular gender. It's just not fair.'

The nanny tells me she's going to break up with her boyfriend. He's nice, but boring. She wants to travel. In fact, she would like to leave soon and do what she's been putting off for so long, which is to spend a year in Australia. Fighting panic, I say well, of course I'll miss you, but I think you should do it. It would be good for you. You've got to take advantage of your freedom while you have it.

She tells me she's never going to give up her freedom. 'I'd like children, but as far as a man is concerned, I'm just not interested.' 'If that's how you feel,' I say, 'you should go back to school and get some more qualifications.' She says she doesn't want to go back to school. 'If you don't and you also don't want to get married, you're going to have a hard time supporting yourself. You don't want to have to go on income support, do you?'

It's clear from her shocked expression that she would never consider it. 'No,' she says, 'I wouldn't dream of sitting at home. I'll always work. After all, I'm a qualified secretary.' I remind her that she will have to spend most of her secretarial salary on childcare. But she remains unimpressed. 'I wouldn't accept a secretarial job unless it paid me properly.' She still doesn't realise that being an exception to the rule takes more than will-power.

My friend Louie tells me that his boyfriend, who teaches at a state secondary school, is getting fed up with the amount of time teachers with children are able to take off in order to take them to the doctor or attend sports days. How can I justify the favouritism? Louie asks me. It's not fair for parents to get time off if no one else gets it. I lose my temper. It's not time off!

Two friends. Both older than I. One tells me about how her daughter is getting frozen out at work. She announced her pregnancy early because she was afraid a friend was going to get made redundant because of her promotion to a position she now won't be wanting quite as soon. Now she's suffering for it. I say how terrible. The other friend, who doesn't have children, says well, it depends on whether it's a job or a career. 'I know you are both going to bite my head off if I tell you this . . .' We say oh go on, we won't bite your head off. She tells us about a friend who became a Woman's Officer in the city council, then had the gall to get pregnant two years later. 'She shouldn't have done that. It was irresponsible. She had a duty to her fellow women to put motherhood off. It took us so long to get contraception and to get taken seriously by the men and now women like this one are ruining it for everyone.'

We bite her head off.

I talk to Heather, a management consultant. Have offer, will travel. She clocks up at least a thousand miles a week. She also teaches whenever the household bills demand. She's just quit a business college because she discovered its operators were crooked. At home it was cause for a champagne candlelit dinner: it was the first weekday night she had spent at home in three and a half months.

I meet up with another old friend, Marion. After sixteen years of bringing up two children on income support, she's back at college to do a degree in French. To supplement the grant, she works as a nanny for a one year old two days a week. The mother is younger than she is. She has a degree in business studies and has managed to negotiate a part-time job for herself at some kind of computer company. Marion doesn't like her very much. She's too fussy. 'If I start a messy game involving pots or water with the child, she comes in and cleans up after me before we're even finished.' She also thinks this woman is not very bright. 'Or perhaps the right word is dull. Or something. I think I find it very difficult to work for a woman who goes off with a briefcase wearing an expensive suit.'

I run into a friend of Frank's at Waitrose. He has his quiet, faintly mistrustful four-year-old daughter with him. He's just returned to university, to do a course in the education school. He's half French and has decided to teach French at secondary level. He has perfect manners.

Until he went back to university, he was looking after his daughter more or less full time. He had difficulty with the social end of things. The other mothers wouldn't trust him. The final rift was when he was the last out of a playgroup yard. He says he remembered closing the gate, but when it was found open later, a number of the women laid into him, and said that it was because of men like him that children in this country were no longer safe.

I'm at home, listening to the news. Esther Rantzen is on again to tell us about how many children ring on behalf of friends. She goes on to talk about what a lonely world it is for many of our nation's children. The impression you get if you're at Childline is that parents today have so little time for their children.

I shout at the radio. 'And why don't you say *why* we have so little time for our children?'

My daughter Emma, who is angry because I didn't let her walk by herself to the newsagent's, says, 'Don't talk to her like that. It's rude. And it's not fair. Esther Rantzen is nice. All she's doing is trying to protect us.' Her eyes add *from you*.

I come across a friend's name while going through my address book. I realise that I haven't heard from him for months and months. I think back to the last time we met. I was going through a crisis at the time, and I confided it all in him. He seemed to be very sympathetic. When I apologised for unloading so much on him, he said it was only fair, as over the years he had done his fair share of confiding in me. That's what friends are for, he said. And that's what we are, aren't we, seeing as we've never slept together?

So why hasn't he been in touch?

I speak to my friend Linda, whose partner is Dan, who is Frank's best friend. Linda is tired, because she's just had to go to the supermarket to buy all the food for the two weeks she'll be away in Africa doing research. Now she's going to have to drive her daughter to her mother's house on the other side of the country.

How's Dan? I ask. Oh, he's fine, she says. He's been working at the kitchen table lately, which is fine with her. The problem is that it is not fine with him that she might need to use the table for some of its normal purposes. 'If I don't clean up as soon as I'm finished, there's hell to pay.'

She's looking forward to her upcoming research trip to Africa.

'He'll be fine here on his own, because he has a lot of work to catch up on. And it's only for five days – after that my mother will come back with Ida and look after both of them until I get back.'

Dan is the only man I know who reads feminist theory. He doesn't just know about the writing, he knows which ones have fanzines, which ones have girlfriends, which ones have boyfriends, and which ones got marginalised in African studies before switching disciplines.

He is a respectable cook but he does not do routine childcare or go to supermarkets.

I've been noticing that my stepson and stepdaughter are pre-occupied. Someone has suggested family counselling. I'm not sure if this is a good idea, but I decide to air it with their mother. She says no, because as far as she's concerned, we're not a family.

I talk to my friend Eleanor, who's seeing a man who's very recently divorced. Two things are distressing her – the amount of time he and his ex-wife spend arguing on the phone, and the attitude he has towards his children. When they're not there, he's always crying about them, and saying he can't live without them, and then, when they are there, he hides behind a newspaper and leaves them to her to look after.

I tell her this sounds pretty standard to me. Wide-eyed, she says, 'It is? But why?'

I talk to Zoë, my old friend from Texas who now lives in El Paso. She's given up on law practice and has gone back to get another degree. She's going to do her thesis on the new anti-illegal immigration legislation in California. 'I feel like I have to. If it weren't for these Mexican women who helped me when Amalia was little, I don't know what I would have done. I could not have survived. So I feel I must fight for them. I owe them at least that.'

It had been a difficult term, though, on account of her mother. She had forced her mother to come back with her from Greece last summer. 'I've been in this country for thirty-five years and no member of my family has ever visited me. So I put my foot down. And so this poor woman went along with it. She had never been off the island before except for a few trips to Athens for medical reasons. And she couldn't take it. When she got to Chicago, she went blind and then psychotic. We got her an operation for her eyes, so eventually she could see again, but she kept on having visions and hearing voices. She was scared out of her wits. I can't tell you how terrifying it was to be holding this chattering woman in my arms. This was a woman I had looked up to all my life. She was so powerful in my eyes, but now she was almost nothing.'

She had recovered the moment she got back to Samos. Now my friend Zoë's problem was her teenage daughter. 'She sat us down at the table the other day, and said hey, you guys, I have something to tell you. I know you were immigrants and you came here and had to work hard. But I'm different. I want to have fun and you guys have to get used to that idea. 'Lefteris and I were stunned. After all we've done, our daughter doesn't fear us.'

Frank's sister sends us another letter. She's fine, and back at work. The baby's fine, almost two months old. She gets up at five every morning and goes to sleep at four-thirty the following morning. She is beginning to feel impatient about these magazine articles that tell you to prepare in advance so that your day can be streamlined. 'When were we supposed to do all this preparing? When we were smoking dope in high school?' The letter is abandoned in mid-sentence, then continued with a differently coloured pen. The PS reads: 'I've decided to stop work even if it means having to give up the house. I feel I owe it to the baby.'

On her next phone call, she says that finances have forced her to increase her hours, but that the more she works, the fatter the baby gets. 'I just don't get it.'

My friend Serena is a doctor. Although she has always worked, she has been ingenious and sometimes even devious about organising her schedule around her three children and their interests. She wants to be the one to collect them from school in the afternoons, the one to take them to sports and pony and ballet lessons. She makes playdates between house visits, organises birthday parties while on call, is never too busy to answer, and answer in painful, patient detail, any question any child might bring to her about the physiology of spiders or the likelihood of a dug-up pottery fragment dating from the Romans. To live like this she has had to sacrifice a conventional career as well as the respectable income that would have accompanied it, but because she has picked up side interests along the way and because these have led to her involvement in projects and studies that she finds far more challenging, she would say that, in the long run, she has gained more than she has lost.

Yes, it is hard to hold all the bits and pieces together, and no, she doesn't know how to relax any more, but at least she has plenty of support. There's her husband, who is an artist, who looked after all three children in the mornings when they were babies. There are her parents, with whom Serena and her family live. Not only do they help out with childcare, but they are also in the habit of benevolently stepping in whenever there is a minor money crisis. And there are her two sisters, who lived with their own families in the same large house until very recently. They are both trained teachers. When they took time off to have their children, they pooled their resources and started a playgroup. Their first charges were Serena's daughter and my daughter. The schedule was informal. Serena's sisters were usually willing to babysit for her at a moment's notice. It's a household in which it's almost impossible to see working and mothering as two separate categories. Each is split into hundreds or even thousands of daily tasks, which the family knits together into its own idiosyncratic routine. All the adults are earners; all share in the responsibility for the children. Or so it seems.

I was visiting Serena a few months ago on the eve of her departure for an international family-planning conference. Her work in the field started as one of many sidelines. Like most of those sidelines, it has grown rather larger than she expected, much to the annoyance of her already overstretched practice partners. To placate them she had been doing double shifts over the two previous weeks. When she handed me my coffee, and told me that this had put her behind schedule, I assumed she meant her conference paper. But it turned out that the document she was poring over was the list of childcare instructions to cover what seemed to be every minute of her absence. Despite the fact that she was handing the children over to five other adults, she had already worked out exactly who drove whom where when, who bought which groceries and how much they would cost. There were numbers for emergencies, lists of schoolfriends with their parents' names and addresses, reminders to pay bills, RSVP invitations, book the car in for an MOT, buy shoes, organise haircuts. She had to write it all down, she said, because otherwise she would return to chaos. It wasn't that she couldn't trust the other members of her family to look after the children. What she couldn't trust them to do was take the initiative. 'Not even Ben.'

I tell her he would if she gave him half a chance. She tells me I'm wrong. 'His game is feigned incompetence.' The last time she ever asked him to make a stew for supper, for example, he added half a pound of tea to it. Serena says that she would prefer to share control, claims that the responsibility that comes with control is a drain on her resources. I tell her she doesn't know how to share control. She says neither do I, and although I have to admit she's right, we keep arguing about it.

Halfway through the argument, Ben arrives. He is too caught up in his own pleasant thoughts to eavesdrop. I look up at the new framed photograph Ben is putting on the wall. He took it a few years ago, when Serena and I were working on a project together. It is of two of our children sound asleep in her study, next to the wood-burning stove, and nestling on a thick, unruly bed of computer paper.

When I get home, I ask Matthew what kind of parent I am. Even as the words leave my lips, I remind myself that this is one more thing my own parents would never have dreamt of doing. 'What kind of *parent* are you?' he muses. 'Hmm. I would say a mixed bag. You're authoritarian when you want something done, and you treat me as an equal when you're bored and don't have anyone else to talk to.' Was he sorry I had told him so much about my private life? 'I think it would be weird to have to spend eighteen years with someone and not know them.' Was he sorry I wasn't perfect? 'I really don't know what to say. I'm not sure I'm in a position to give you a balanced answer. Maybe you could introduce me to a perfect mother first so that I can find out what they're like.'

My daughter Emma has recently gone haywire over Take That. She has plastered her walls with posters of them. Going in there is like going into a gay bar. The other weekend, when she was away with her father, I had some friends to stay. I put their three year old in Emma's bedroom. The girl had to be switched to another room halfway through the night, because the posters were giving her nightmares.

Emma asked me to take her over to a friend's house. The friend was holding a *Blue Peter* bring-and-buy sale. As I was standing outside talking to the mother, another woman walked by complaining about the fête at the local primary school. 'Four hundred children and they couldn't find enough parents to run a cake stall!' this woman said. 'It makes you wonder why they had children at all.' I suggested that the parents were probably exhausted after working sixty-hour weeks. The two women shook their heads. 'It's a question of attitude. If you want to help out, you always find the time.'

I considered trying to explain to them that this is dealing with the symptom instead of looking at the root cause, but decided it wasn't fair, not polite, and so not right. I switched the conversation to the controversial bypass that was under construction on the other side of the valley. From here you had a clear view of it. Both women said they had a hard time even looking out of their windows. 'It's so upsetting watching them build yet another road, because it's dealing with the symptom instead of the root problem.'

My friend Ellen is in distress. After working a ten-hour day, she stayed up until half-past one to make a chocolate log for her children's school. She says she feels mistrusted by the full-time mothers, and wanted to prove herself and perhaps win their approval. It turned out that all the other mothers brought shop-bought snacks. The chocolate log was an anomaly. 'I felt such a fool.'

I was once rejected by a group of Other Mothers because my child stood on top of a playhouse and said, 'Fuck fuck fuck.' Another budding friendship ended when the other mother tried to get me to go on an est weekend. I lost another new friend when I put the stereo on too loud not long after revealing that I did not save milk-bottle tops for Oxfam.

But it works both ways. I lost hope about one mother when I discovered she was trying to wean her child from breast milk to water and the odd banana. A second because she slapped my daughter Emma for wetting her pants. Another playdate turned to dust when Emma told the potential friend's mother that she'd lost Jesus. Not knowing that this was the name of Emma's doll, or that the name had been acquired by virtue of the doll having appeared in a Nativity play, the mother was aghast – especially when Emma returned to announce to her that she had now *found* Jesus.

I taught my children to be wary of arbitrary authority. I taught them that parents weren't perfect and sometimes behaved childishly – even if they tried not to. The message has got through to them. The problem is that *they* almost *never* feel childish. Why should they, when their vote counts for as much as ours does? They know what their rights and entitlements are. Having been encouraged to think for themselves, they do. This is all to the good, but it creates procedural problems. Children who are first-class citizens don't follow instructions, not even in an emergency. They stop in their tracks and ask why, and refuse to budge until they have accepted your request as reasonable. This can be dangerous (as, for example, in heavy traffic) and even impossible (when, like any overworked parent, you want them to do something like clear the table simply because you don't feel like doing it yourself).

A certain hypocritical note creeps into these explanations, especially when you're trying to explain sex or violence or poverty or war or death. ('Yes, of course you will, darling, certainly not tonight because I'm here watching over you!') Trained egalitarian children become good at detecting the contradictions in your full disclosures. ('Of course it's not your fault we're getting divorced! It's just that we haven't been able to get along since we had children!') This leads inexorably to more and longer discussions – and better little debaters. Lecture an equal child for refusing to do his homework, and you'll hear what the suicide rate is amongst overworked pupils in Japan. Tell an equal child to eat her free lunch, and she'll soon be undermining your position with the latest findings on anorexia. They also have a terrible habit of using their large information-base against their liberators. ('Why should *we* try to get along when you and Daddy aren't even *speaking*?') And they feel insulted, even betrayed, if ever you have the nerve to take them to a place where they are not the centre of attention. ('What am I doing at this dinner party anyway? No one's talking to *me*.')

'From dawn till dusk, all I do is answer questions!' as one friend put it. 'Explain this to me. Explain that to me. And then, after I have talked myself silly, they won't take my word for it!' In the early years, our children's little antics were light entertainment. I used to laugh, for example, at the sight of the three-year-old daughter and her best friend changing Darth Vader's nappy. I was almost proud when, about a year later, they decided, after careful weighing of the evidence, that God might be everywhere, but not in shoes or Sainsbury's. I was amused when my daughter asked me what the difference was between a normal fax and the fax of life; when my stepdaughter asked her father where the pole tacks lived, and when she told an uncle that she thought John Major was dangerous because he was always driving down the middle of the road. I felt just a bit for staid house-guests who were queried about the shape and number of their genitals, and also for a nice retired lady of my acquaintance whose grandson paused in the middle of a rapturous thanksgiving for the peas she had made for him ('I love these peas! I want to marry these peas!') to ask, 'Do peas have vaginas?'

It was embarrassing, but yes, amusing when they took to singing 'Happiness Is a Warm Gun' in the queue at Mothercare, and deeply satisfying when they tried my favourite swear words out on a hated dentist. But expletives are not as funny when they're addressing you at eye-level – especially when they fend off any suggestion that they should stop with a threat to ring Childline.

I suppose I was just as good at looking after my interests when I was their age. But I certainly didn't expect them to have quite so much variety. My Christmas lists were generic: dolls, I suggested hopefully. Books. Games. A list I got recently read: 'Robocop II. Bubble Jet Printer BJ-10ex. Five trolls, including the one in the nurse's outfit. Assorted small blue Wedgwood collectibles. One Sony portable TV.' When I explained that we were going to have to trim things down this year, the child said, 'Then I'll be happy with just the Sony portable TV.'

Yes, television. Television has worked hand in hand with egalitarian parents to arm children with information that will save them from disease, bad environmental habits, products tested on animals and their evil elders. But there is nothing quite as strange as health awareness combined with small vocabularies or eco-consciousness grafted on to political innocence. My children knew what the word 'condom' meant long before they could pronounce the word 'relationship'. They wouldn't dream of judging someone by his skin, but they hate, hate, hate countries that destroy their own rain forests or condone the killing of whales.

Their awareness of perversion outstrips their understanding of the normal. There was a time, for example, when my son assumed that any three adults living together in the same house were a *ménage à trois*. There was another time when I walked into the kitchen to find my son and my daughter and four or five of their friends doubled over with laughter, the way my friends and I used to be when we made trick telephone calls, or did practical jokes involving fake love letters. It turned out that they were drafting fake incest confessions, complete with (to them) hilarious spelling mistakes, for a magazine agony aunt. 'I was eight and a harf when my stepfather began to fondle me in a family way,' began one. Another went, 'After he put It back in his troosers, he said he'd kill me if I ever told anybody.'

Despite their sophisticated vocabulary, their world is still divided between the good guys and the bad guys. I remember the last election, when I found Emma, then eight, in tears in her bed, sobbing, 'Why oh why do we have to live in Douglas Hurd country?' Their eyes are old but their imaginations are young. Unspeakable nightmares lurk everywhere. I cite as an example one friend's son's hysteria on being handed his first roll of recycled loo paper. *We* know it's from nice, clean recycled business correspondence. *He* thought it had been fished out of the sewage system.

But at least his mother doesn't have to worry about having robbed these children of their childhoods. Not a chance. They're too selfish. This same boy who was traumatised by the loo paper, for example, had to write an essay in conjunction with a class project on Martin Luther King. The question was: Have you ever stood up for something you believed in and suffered for it? It was his mother's turn to be aghast when she discovered he had written about asking to gallop on his sister's pony, and being told he couldn't, and standing in the stirrups and making it gallop anyway, and falling off the pony, and getting hurt, thereby suffering for it.

Slowly and reluctantly, my friends and I are beginning to discover what everyone else probably knew all along – that equality isn't necessarily educational. And can be dangerous. It's one thing to tell children to respect their own opinions and express themselves and move beyond the narrow moulds of gender. It's quite another to send these children, with their misplaced confidence, out into a hierarchical world that rewards obedience and conformity to those same narrow moulds of gender. As one recovering egalitarian put it, 'You go along, during those happy years when you're teaching them to think independently, but still running the show, because you're bigger and stronger than they are, and then, suddenly one day, out the door they go, expecting to be able handle anything, and you realise, too late, that the point of having some authority over your children is to protect them.'

This is our everyday world. Men are not men here. Women are not women. Children are not children. Homes are not stable.

Jobs are not for life. Marriages end. New ones begin. And it's hard even to find a friend who agrees with you about anything. This is a world in which nothing can be taken for granted, in which people have changed but usually only halfway or half the time, and where everything, but everything, must be renegotiated almost daily.

Children are sometimes born inside wedlock in this multiple-choice Babylon, and sometimes without. Husbands cook but don't shop. Or shop but get out of cooking by making stews with tea-leaves. Wives shop but go to Africa to do research. Or never shop because they're never home. Women without children take against women with children. Women with children take against men with children. Mothers who stay at home think unkindly about mothers who don't. Ten year olds who have never been allowed to cross the road without their mothers cannot understand why their parents cannot discuss sex with their grandparents.

Mothers still envy daughters. Daughters still resent mothers. Children still argue about whose father is stronger, except that now they are more likely to get to the heart of things and use the word 'penis'. But things have changed here in family land. There is no paradise of mother-and-child dyads, no uniform standard of gender formation. The days of motor-driven patriarchal value-transmission are gone, if they ever existed. I do not understand what I see instead, but here I am one up on the social planners and political thinkers and even most of our feminist theorists: *they* don't even see it.

The invisible burden

That's the name of the game. And the root cause of our everyday problems. Not only is our domestic work unpaid: it must be done invisibly. Once upon a time it was expected, at least amongst the middle classes, that it would be done invisibly by a woman who did not also have to earn a living. Now, working mothers and fathers face the challenge of doing the same diffuse, unpredictable and complicated job in a fraction of the time and, like Olympic gymnasts, never show the strain. Their performances may be less than perfect, but their standards have not fallen accordingly. Contrary to popular opinion, parents, whether they work or not, really do try to do what economists have expected families to do, which is to absorb the shocks of rapid change while offering its members some degree of protection. It shouldn't be surprising that their private contortions go unnoticed and uncelebrated, because that is the whole point.

Why does it have to be like this? According to economist Diane Elson, it's because few if any planners give due importance to unpaid labour:

> Of course, when challenged, economists do not deny that sustaining and reproducing a labour force relies on unpaid inputs of cooking and caring, nurturing and nourishing; and that variations in this input may play a significant role in adjustment processes. But they do not see the need to take this explicitly into account when modelling the functioning of the macro economy. In effect, they behave as if such unpaid labour can be taken for granted, and treated as readily available in whatever quantities are required regardless of changes in the composition, or level, or distribution of national income.

She traces several problems to this abuse of unpaid labour. While it may be true that women and families do usually manage to meet their unpaid responsibilities in times of crisis and so 'cushion the process of adjustment', this effort jeopardises women's health and morale. Where they have to pass responsibilities on to their daughters, they are forced to interrupt, or curtail, their daughters' education. When they do not have daughters to take up the slack, and their domestic responsibilities impinge on their work day, they will either not be able to work or will only be able to turn up irregularly. And when the double load becomes too much to handle, 'things fall apart in the household and the community, with potentially serious repercussions for economic, social, and political stability'.[6]

She cites a study of Zambia,[7] where real per capita health expenditure fell by 16 per cent between 1983 and 1985. For most Zambians, the only alternatives to state health care were 'the community and household – which in practice means women'. This obligation affected their own performance in the paid labour market:

> Women interviewed for the study said they themselves could not afford to be ill because of the time it would take away from their work. They reported having to spend more time caring for other household members when they are sick. If husbands and children have to attend hospitals, shortages of equipment and personnel mean that women are expected to go with them to provide meals and care for the duration of the treatment. One woman reported missing the entire planting season for this reason, a perfect example of the interdependence between the labour that macro-economic models do include and that which they ignore.[8]

Ignoring these things, she says, is:

> . . . tantamount to assuming that women's capacity to undertake extra work is infinitely elastic – able to stretch so as to make up for any shortfall in incomes and resources required for the production and maintenance of human resources. However, women's capacity for work is not infinitely elastic and breaking-point may be reached. There may simply not be enough female labour time available to maintain the quality and quantity of human resources at its existing level.[9]

To support her point, she draws upon a study that traced the adjustments women in an urban low-income community in Ecuador had to make after the economy introduced hardship measures to weather an international economic slump. These women's paid and unpaid working days:

> . . . continued to be between twelve and eighteen hours, but they had been forced to reduce the time allocated to looking after their families. An increasing burden was falling on the shoulders of their elder daughters, who had less time for school work . . . Total input of female labour time had increased, though since adult women already

worked very long hours, much of the extra input was coming from school-age daughters. In about 30 per cent of the 141 households surveyed, women were managing to cope; in about 55 per cent, women were just hanging on, mortgaging the futures of their sons, and especially their daughters, in order to survive; in about 15 per cent, women were exhausted, their families disintegrating, their children dropping out of school and roaming the streets, becoming involved in street gangs and exposed to drugs. As Moser concludes, 'Not all women can cope under crisis and it is necessary to stop romanticising their infinite capacity to do so.'[10]

Diane Elson believes that macroeconomic strategy could become more reliable (and benefit everyone, not just women) if it paid more attention to the complicated ways in which paid and unpaid labour interact:

A focus on unpaid as well as paid labour highlights the issue of use of time as a key, but often neglected, quality-of-life indicator. How many hours are spent in work rather than leisure? How far can people *choose* the amount of time they devote to work for a particular length of time? How intensively do people work, when they are working? What is the distribution of working time between different members of the population?[11]

Even though unpaid work and leisure overlap, it is important not to conflate unpaid work, which has 'an element of social service' and leisure, 'which might be defined as self-centred'. 'We all need and deserve some time for ourselves but we also all need others to undertake unpaid work for us.' It is also important to distinguish between voluntary unpaid work, which carries some social status and affords certain powers, and the house and childcare work that is, in most houses in most parts of the world:

... the social obligation of women, either to undertake it themselves if they are poorer, or to hire and supervise servants to underake it, if they are richer. Women who refuse or neglect this obligation are 'bad' women, subject to, at best, social disapproval and criticism, and at worst, domestic violence.[12]

She does not advocate assigning a numerical value to the work they do, rather, looking into ways in which strategies can be designed so as to take into account the work women do, and the time they need to do it:

> At the heart of any democratic and egalitarian strategy must be a carefully designed public expenditure programme that serves to increase the productivity of both paid and unpaid labour. Unpaid labour should not be seen as a substitute for public expenditure. Rather public expenditure should be seen as a way of transforming and increasing the effectiveness of unpaid labour.[13]

Needless to say, this is not happening in Zambia, or in Ecuador, and it is not happening here. What is happening here, and in the US, and all over the developed world, is a huge influx of women into a service sector vastly enlarged by computerisation. Meanwhile, unions have been less than successful in providing the sort of social and economic supports that these new working women, so many of whom are also mothers, need in order to work in secure nine-to-five jobs. This lack of support has increased the pool of women willing to work part time or at odd hours that fit in with their family obligations. These jobs, which suit employers fine and so are proving more and more popular, are low paid, and often exist beyond the scope of employment law. Barring aggressive political intervention, they are likely to remain so.

If you want the unbelievably depressing facts about the earnings of working women in this country, the type of childcare that is available to them, and the type of protection they can expect from equal opportunity legislation during pregnancy and after, I direct your attention to *Because of Her Sex* by Kate Figes. She reports that of the 11 million women in employment, four and a half million work part time. Three and a half million of these are mothers. About a third of mothers returning to work full time after the birth of their first child end up switching to part-time work:

> because of the strain of maintaining both responsibilities. Flexibility is sold as the main perk, and as an advantage which somehow mitigates the drawbacks of low pay, low status, little employmen protection, next to no training and limited prospects for promotion[14] . . . The increased use of flexible labour, with lower pay and almost negligible conditions, can be found in every area of employment where there are women in substantial numbers – in nursing and teaching, in the leisure industry, for example cinemas and bingo halls, in retailing, in banking and in building societies.[15]

It can also be found, dare I add, in such prestige middle-class bastions as newspapers and publishing.

> It is now estimated that half of all working women in Britain – more than twice the number of men – are employed on atypical contracts describing them as part time, temporary, or self-employed. There is another hidden advantage to this trend, for the Public Sector Borrowing Requirement. Without the benefits of sick and maternity pay, unemployment benefit or a full state pension, these women will draw less on the welfare state, being forced back on to a male earner for support.[16]

That is, assuming he's there.

And, that is, without even mentioning childcare. State nurseries only exist for the neediest children. Despite the lipservice paid to the idea of workplace nurseries, there are only 425 of them in this country. Because school schedules are not designed to fit in with the schedules of full-time employment, the childcare problem persists after children are in full-time education. 'Our *ad hoc*, cheapskate approach to childcare is perpetuating divided opportunities for women; it is also contributing to the polarisation of resources and capabilities of the next generation.'[17]

Women, Figes says, are being punished for their desire for children. It is rarely acknowledged that, in choosing to bring up a child, they are performing a valuable service. The idea that a mother's small pay packet makes her children suffer is not one our right-wing politicians like to dwell upon. It is even more rarely acknowledged that the cheap labour she provides as a result of her inability to find affordable childcare does also pose a threat to childless people in full-time jobs. In a marketplace where there are ever fewer jobs for life, a cheap labour pool of part-time workers in a given industry undermines the bargaining power of its full-time workers. It is no accident, I would say, that the growth of part-time and contract employment is occurring at the same time as the trend towards skeleton staffs in which full-time workers find themselves doing jobs that used to require the services of two or even three people.

People who know they can be replaced, and know they can't depend on the law to protect them, can't getting picky about job descriptions, can't stand on principle, and can't bargain. For mothers who work, this problem exists right across the board, and I mean from the rice paddy to the executive suite.

They must add to a weak power base a second problem – they are paid less, again across the board, because it is assumed they are dependants. But this is no longer true. While we were marching idealistically for the right to work during the sixties and seventies, something strange happened to average real earnings. Or rather didn't happen. Average real earnings in the US, for example, have remained static for twenty years. A household that could have survived on a single income in the early seventies now needs a dual income. Work is not the optional extra we may once have thought it was. But the people who design the workplace, and the school system, and just about every other system, still pretend that each family can afford a stay-at-home mother.

The effects of this institutional intransigence on low-paid workers are generally known – at least in the plural. Out there somewhere in the nation's ugly neighbourhoods, there are hundreds of thousands of working mothers who barely earn enough to pay the childminder. They are caught in the traps, people say, because they don't have enough education.

It would follow from this that, if you do have education, you are in a position to 'change the work culture' to meet your needs.

This was the idea Deborah J. Swiss and Judith P. Walker had in mind when they set out to interview 902 women graduates of Harvard's Business, Medical and Law Schools for their book, *Women and the Work/Family Dilemma*. What they wanted to find out was what these resourceful and assertive high achievers had done to balance home and work. The hope was that the rest of us could learn from them. Instead the authors stumbled into a nightmare. Although 96 per cent of the Harvard high achievers had returned to work before their first child was a year old, and 82 per cent in less than four months, 53 per cent had had to change jobs due to 'family reasons'. These 'reasons' included twelve-hour days, twenty-four-hour-a-day availability to clients and superiors, compulsory travel, no time off for children's illnesses – and continuing suspicion and discrimination even when they played by these rules, especially during pregnancy.

Of the women interviewed, 85 per cent believed that to go part time was to kill your career. Even so, 70 per cent had resorted to part-time work to ease the pressure of 'trying to build coherence where it has never existed',[18] Just about everyone spoke of something being missing in their lives. The story that sticks in my mind is the hard-driving single businesswoman mother whose six month old had to undergo surgery for a brain tumour. When she looked for moral support, she found she had only one friend.

When these women set out to have families as well as careers, they thought they were helping all women, not just themselves, by creating role models and breaking through traditional barriers. They have more than done their homework. For twenty years now, Swiss and Walker say, working mothers:

> ... have done all of the accommodating in terms of time, energy, and personal sacrifice that is humanly possible, and still they have not reached true integration in the workplace. [Instead they] find themselves in an intense battle with a society that cannot let go of a narrowly defined work ethic that is supported by a family structure that has not existed for decades.[19]

The glass ceiling is firmly in place in the US – if change continues at its current rate, the integration of the executive suite will take 475 years. Meanwhile, 56 per cent of mothers with children under six, and 73 per cent of women with children over six are in the work force.[20] That most of them are exploited is a truism. That they do not suffer alone, but share the hardships with their partners and their children, is not a truism, but it ought to be.

Certainly, this is a message that comes through in every case history of the Harvard best and brightest. Most of these women look as if they're coping well, but all that means is that they've learned how to keep their taut, overscheduled, and so impoverished, home lives invisible. When they describe how they pull off the conjuring trick, they describe a world I know: a world where pregnancy is suspect, where taking maternity leave means risking the sack, where staying at home with the baby means working while the baby is on the breast, where women who can't afford time off and can't find childcare smuggle newborns into the office and hide them under the desk, a world where half of a woman's already proportionately lower pay packet will go to pay for substandard childcare; where she does six hours at home after eight hours at the office, if she's lucky enough to have an office; where, in order to attend a school play or take a child to the doctor, she feels obliged to lie and say she's going to a chiropractor for her back. A world where you spend your best energy coping with people who refuse to cope with you.

And the costs of purgatory are high, as Dr Arlie Hochschild proves in devastating detail in a study of working parents called *The Second Shift*. As a social scientist, she is well aware that it takes more than a book about rotten fifties suburbs to get a social revolution going. It was, she reminds us, the changing economy that created the need for our new gender ideology, with its egalitarian code of honour and identity. But even though the 'gender revolution is caused by changes in the economy, people *feel* it in marriage'.[21] They feel it a lot more, too, if social and political institutions fail to reflect these same changes in the economy. In the more enlightened parts of Europe, there have been social and political adjustments that reflect the needs of the new workforce and the new family. But here, and in the US, they are few and far between.

The result is what she calls a 'stalled revolution'. Swiss and Walker call it the continuation of the same old problem:

> Discrimination of women in the workplace because of gender ... or because of the decision to become a mother ... has taken a less visible course ... but it is more insidious and more immune to recourse.'[22]

Echoing Diane Elson, they point out that the results are not just damaging to women and their families, but to business and society:

> Not only does the unnecessary collision between careers and children take a personal toll of family life, it also affects productivity by alienating people from their companies and professions. By making it difficult for half the work population to use their skills and talents fully, business is penalising itself and jeopardising its future growth.[23]

What we need to do, they say, is to force the workplace to change, and thoroughly, so that victories don't all evaporate through loopholes and inequities. They warn that this will not happen if parents content themselves with individual solutions. Instead they call for all parents to work collectively to overhaul the workplace and the laws that govern it.

If we took this call seriously, it would mean working together with other parents, first to understand and evaluate what we do, and to define what we do *in our own terms*, to agree on what basic conditions parents and children and other dependants deserve in a humane society, and then to fight for them.

It would probably also mean being part of a larger effort to set better standards that take into account the time and energy and security all working people need to set aside for their home commitments. Standards that reflect the view that time off paid work is not necessarily time off work. That recognise that a protected space for private life, whatever form it takes, is not just necessary for people's welfare and sanity, but essential if they are to work productively.

The public world would not survive without the unpaid work we do privately for our families and our friends and our communities. We are all in the same boat: men, women, earners, dependants, child-laden and child-free. We are all suffering across the board and throughout the world from the present anachronistic arrangements for paid and unpaid labour. We could use this awareness to put behind past betrayals and work together, at least on this problem, for the common good. We could. So far we haven't. Why?

Part Three

The World From the Margins

8

A BLEAK PICTURE

Why are feminists so wary of the family?

Families are not just about sexism. That is the problem with families from the feminist point of view.

If, like Elizabeth V. Spelman,[1] you think feminism should do more than just analyse gender, surely there could be no better way to support your argument than to point to the complexity and diversity of the families in which most women live today. But there has been no such renaissance. Although there are acres of feminists who have done interesting and valuable studies of all nature of families, their insights rarely carry over into general feminist discussions of the Institution of Motherhood as it exists inside the Patriarchal Family.

Why have our great feminist thinkers been so reluctant to look beyond this giant boulder, this overblown balloon cartoon of a concept? Why has no serious thinker pointed out the patently obvious – that the Institution of Motherhood as it is meant to exist inside the Patriarchal Family is a big, fat, idiotic myth? Even socialist feminists, who have written so consistently about class and race as well as gender, seem unable to think of the family as anything but enemy territory. Even those nostalgic accounts of those early seventies communes seem to confirm the prevailing suspicion that a woman's family ties are always and disastrously at odds with her feminist aspirations. And yet, if you bother to look carefully at the so-called feminist canon, you can find plenty of passages in plenty of books that indirectly challenge this suspicion.

You do not have to give up your feminist ideas in order to speak out in defence of parents, children and families. To do so

189

intelligently, you'll need better developed ideas than the ones on offer now, but that doesn't mean you have to start from scratch. You could do worse than start with Mary O'Brien.[2] She, you may remember, was the one who said that the new freedom to be able to choose and time motherhood was forcing women to the political arena in a way unprecedented in history. She predicted that the political battles over fertility were going to be where the action was in the century to come. When she said that women needed a new political theory to cope with birth control, by birth control she did not just mean the right not to conceive, she also meant the right *to* conceive. She meant the right to have some say over what happens to the children that result, and the kind of life you have if you choose to be a mother – and so did Julia Kristeva when she made her passionate call for a new ethics of maternity in her famous 1977 essay, 'Stabat Mater'.

Her view was that the decline in Catholic countries of the cult of the Virgin, and elsewhere of religion in general, had left us with no way to solve the problem of 'feminine paranoia'. No way, in other words, to understand our place as women in the world, or our desire to have children, or indeed our place as mothers in the scheme of things – in myth, in religion, and in history. No way to grow up. To create a 'postvirginal' discourse on maternity:

> . . . one needs to listen, more carefully than ever, to what mothers are saying today, through their economic difficulties and, beyond the guilt that a too existentialist feminism handed down, through their discomforts, insomnias, joys, angers, desires, pains and pleasures.[3]

Although her later writing has remained vague and circumspect about the shape this discourse might take, the maternal thinker Sara Ruddick has defined it rigorously.[4] She, you may remember, is the one who dared to suggest that mothering required intelligence. Not everyone could be expected to share her optimism about the possible pacifist uses of maternal thinking. But in arguing that maternal thinking can become political thinking, she provides a grounding for two radical suggestions that many

Difference Feminists have suggested but never insisted upon – one, that certain very valuable forms of thinking begin at home, and two, that these forms of thinking can be, and desperately need to be, extended beyond the home to challenge and become integrated with traditional political thinking.

A domestic ethic is not necessarily an ethic that enslaves women. That's what Jean Bethke Elshtain argues in *Public Man/Private Woman*. She makes a case for a family that can be a force of social change instead of an impediment to it, and a private realm that protects families and children without stepping all over women. By sifting through the prevailing ideas of public and private from the Greeks to the present, she confirms our current suspicions about the word private being a euphemism used to justify shutting women out of public life. But she also shows what happens when political theory refuses to distinguish between the private and the public realms. When public life must follow the family ethic, or when politicians feel no need to respect family privacy, what we are looking at, she says, is fascism, or totalitarianism, or patriarchal government in its purest form. And what we are destroying is the possibility for democratic pluralism.

The question that concerns her most is not how to imagine a better world, but how to get from here to there. Do you impose your superior system on people who must be forced to be free? If you don't, if you think that's wrong, where is the best place for people to take refuge from the corrupt world while they struggle to put their fine ideas into practice? She suggests it is a family in a reconceived private realm, where people could make mistakes without becoming immediate pawns in political struggles, could work out, detail, by detail, which traditions they wanted to keep, which they wanted to alter slightly, and which they could do without altogether. She also suggests that it is only through establishing close, rich ties with adults inside families that humans become human. Citing the Wolf Boy of Aveyron as an example of what happens in a world where children are not nurtured, she calls for 'the redemption of everyday life, its joys and vexation, its values and purposes, and its place in becoming human'.[5]

We need to communicate, she says, but we also need to

conceal. A world without shadows or hiding places is a world in which Nazis have no trouble keeping control. Instead of:

> ... overpoliticising our most intimate relations and turning the family into the war of all against all to be negotiated by contract [we should be] fighting the pressures at work from the outside which erode, impoverish, or preclude the flourishing of our most basic human ties.[6]

Feminists can protect the family space, in other words, without automatically reinforcing that clumsy old warhorse, the Institution of Motherhood. Likewise, mothers do not have to give up on a public role just because they have a private role. That's the idea behind *Mothers and Modernity*, in which Christine Everingham goes to heroic lengths to rescue the private realm of mothers, children and families from its present obscurity by redefining it as a second sphere of action. This is in daring contrast to what it has traditionally been in modern thought, the passive anchor where nothing changes and nothing intelligent ever happens. She wants to prove that mothers don't just think, but think together, and construct their own ideologies instead of just transmitting those handed down to them from on high. Not quite alone of all her sex, but almost, she believes that the society of mothers can work collectively, and around their specific needs at the grassroots level, while also representing those same needs and interests in a more general way at the political level.[7]

These writers' ideas might not be at the top of the feminist agenda, but they are still there, part of the canon. Waiting, like Rapunzel, to be released from the ivory tower. Why doesn't the general public even know they're there?

Because they don't fit in with the fairy-tale logic of sexual politics

By which I do not mean to say that sexual politics hasn't got its uses. After all, it has kept the word 'feminism' in the news while also providing us with excellent entertainment. I mean – who wants to watch the painfully slow and desperately confusing spectacle of undirected social change, or the separation of gender facts from gender fictions, when you can watch wicked men and pure women argue about pornography, when the courts are full of diverting rape, incest, divorce and harassment trials? Who wants to agonise over the consequences of half-baked feminist ideas that yield disturbing results when put into practice, when you can blame all evil on patriarchs and just prance through life repressing, resisting, and reshaping them? Why think and worry in a plotless world, if, like Dworkin and MacKinnon, you can see one plot wherever you look?

Come one, come all. It's the greatest show on earth, greater than Oedipus Rex, greater even than Genesis. It's the greatest come-on ever invented.

Come and see if this time, finally, Adam will get fucked by his rib!

Every sensational trial, every man-hating feminist bestseller, every tabloid article denigrating liberated women, is an attempt to boil life down into this apparently simple formula. Its downmarket equivalent, also popular in newspapers, as well as pubs and locker rooms, is the gender game. Which is sort of like eating popcorn. Once you start, it's hard to stop. If something's bad because it's traditionally male, is its traditionally female opposite good? When should a woman be more like a man, and when should she be herself? If she is more like a man, though, isn't she herself already? If all men have a female side, can anyone call men men, or women women?

In her feminist classic, *Thinking About Women*, Mary Ellmann suggested that human beings could not think without resorting to sexual analogy. 'If a wounded tribesman lying on the ground watched a large, round cloud cross the sky, he would die thinking: That cloud is pregnant.'[8] But now that technology and feminism have rescued sexuality from fertility, things have changed. Now he would say: That cloud is asking for it, or: That cloud is frigid. While the cloud would say: I'll define my own boundaries, thank you very much, and in the meantime, keep out of my space. When sexuality becomes something entirely separate from procreation, we quickly lose sight of the idea that there might be one project that both sexes can embark on together. We only get the other half of the story. We only hear about the competition.

Does feminist sexual analogy always have to be domination and subjugation? Cultural feminists like Helen Haste would say no.[9] The problem with our sexual metaphors now, she says, is that the male and the female versions cancel each other out. She suggests new metaphors that live and let live – and so does Lynne Segal. In her new book on straight sex, she says that we all know, every time we have sex, that there is a huge gap between what we feel and what we want and what we get in bed and what our rigid sexual ideology suggests we ought to feel, want, and get. She says that we cling to this ideology none the less because it gives us the security of a clear framework.[10]

This is what popular sexual politics does too. On the surface, and alas, only on the surface, it provides us with the simple plots, stock characters, and clear outcomes we need in order to work out how to match our changing conditions with our ideas of right and wrong.

But at the same time, because it is a fairy-tale inversion of reality, it's blinded us to what's really been happening. Because it is dominated not by the puppet figures on the surface, but by the unnamed fears lurking in the background, it's exacerbated these fears. And because these fears have clouded our reason, the fairy-tale of sexual politics has mangled our understanding of mothers, fathers, children, families, and just about any association between two people that doesn't involve, or doesn't just involve, sex. It's caused us to see sex where there isn't any, turned us into a confederation of paranoid fantasists.

It may well be that there is a secret world out there in which all men are molesters at home, harassers at the office, and want their women in one place and one place only – under their thumb. I would say this is about as likely as the ideal image it replaced – of a world in which all men were good husbands, wise fathers, and trustworthy employers. If that world of patriarchal perfection existed only in the mind to serve the dominant ideology, then the same could be true of the nightmare world conjured up by sexual politicians.

He dominates, she succumbs. She resists, he retaliates. He and she go to the public with two versions of events that cancel each other out. I would not presume to guess what it all means, but I would suggest that it would make a lot more sense if you entertained the possibility that the drama might have more than the two characters in the foreground. That sexual politics might not just be about men trying to dominate women. That lurking in the background behind every seesaw allowing a man mostly to dominate and obliging a woman mostly to succumb is another shadowy figure who aids and abets.

Consider, for example, the classic incest scenario which has acted so powerfully on the collective feminist imagination: the wicked father who abuses the innocent daughter. Where is the mother in this picture? Why isn't she protecting the girl, and challenging the abuser? All too often she is the one whose absence or inaction make the abuse possible. All too often she is the silent partner who has abandoned the daughter to the father, whose willed ignorance or collusion makes the wicked seduction possible. All too often it is said that she colludes because she can imagine no other way, because she has no real power, because her own mother abandoned her in the same way. But that doesn't make the crime any lighter, or the daughter's sense of betrayal any easier to bear. More to the point, it doesn't make it any easier for feminist sexual politicians to see the maternal tradition in any terms other than betrayal.

Which is pretty funny if you step back and look at the big picture, because what's really happened is that *they've* betrayed *us*

I am talking now about these altermaters who lured me and so many others into feminism, only to abandon us when our problems became too adult for their adolescent frame of reference. When we left the foreground of their favourite fairy-tale, and walked into a pair of shoes they were too afraid to retrieve from the shadows.

Why did they seduce us in the first place if they didn't intend to see us through? *Why* have they abandoned us? Why do they refuse even to admit that this is what they've done?

It has taken me most of my life to work out that I am never

going to get satisfactory answers to these questions unless I answer them myself. Unless I accept that I expected too much. If I feel betrayed by the feminist movement, it's not because of the emptiness of its original promises, but because I put too much trust in a collection of ideas that were, like all ideas everywhere, not as reliable as advertised. And as the Jungian James Hillman pointed out in his essay on betrayal, trust is not the most mature of emotions. Trust is what babies feel, and what adults can only relive when they have managed to fool themselves back into the false security of babyhood. Trust is what you feel when you first fall in love, when you've made a new friend who seems to know you perfectly, when you give yourself over to a new idea. It's a return, he would say, to the Garden of Eden, to the bliss you felt in the arms of your mother before you worked out that these arms did not exist for the sole purpose of holding you. Whenever you are dropped, abandoned, misused by someone you put your trust in, the sting you feel is the sting you felt the first time your mother failed to play her part in your antelapsarian fantasy.[11] And if the person who let you down was someone who had deliberately set out to act like a mother and make you feel like a daughter, then the sting can only grow sharper.

Hence, I would imagine, my excessive rage against my altermaters, my unreasonable desire to hold them responsible for everything. At the same time I know that their political failures were no more deliberate than my personal failures, and what's more, that there are very good reasons for these political failures. Reasons that are so good that they made these failures almost inevitable. But not, by the same token, impossible to remedy.

If you can't understand why something has gone wrong, then you'll waste the rest of your life stuck in a rut and wondering. If you can conjure up even the sketchiest understanding, if you can put yourself in your forerunners' shoes and understand that they were doing the best they could within the limits of their own understanding, then there is a chance you might be able to get out of the rut and move on. So this is what I'm trying to do — come up with my own explanation as to why these women allowed themselves to forget we existed, and why this new generation of feminist popstars has been content to continue the pretence. I want an explanation that is more than an accusation, less than a cry of abandonment. An explanation that takes their perspectives into account without cancelling out my own. In which my side of the story and their sides of the story combine to explain what neither story can explain on its own – why we remain locked inside the Oedipal logic of sexual politics, why feminism has proved so powerless against what French psychoanalyst Monique Plaza calls the 'vast apparatus of hatred of the Mother'[12] – and how this nightmare drama has hampered our every effort to bring about real social and political change.

I'll kick off with Julia Kristeva, who explains it like this: we live in a civilization, she says, where femininity equals motherhood. But this idea of motherhood that femininity equals has nothing to do with maternal work. Instead it is 'the *fantasy* that is nurtured by the adult, man or woman, of a lost territory'. This is the lost territory of innocence, the impossibly idealised memory of the perfect mother-and-child bond, of perfect trust. The mistake feminists have made, she says, is to fall for the fantasy even as they reject it – to assume that mothers are really as we all perceive them.[13] I would go on to suggest that feminists have had a hard time identifying this mistake because the feminism itself is grounded in a particularly virulent form of this same fantasy – of paradise lost, of perfect trust broken, of mothers turned treacherous, and children abandoned.

This fantasy finds its most beautiful expression in feminism's own creation myth, *Frankenstein*

Or perhaps it would be more correct to call *Frankenstein* the myth that best expresses the mood of second-wave feminism, which, as so many writers have noted, is quintessentially a 'daughter's revolution'. As peace activist Ynestra King put it:

> Even when mothers join the movement it is often the wronged daughter in them who speaks. Each of us is familiar as daughters with maternal practice, but most of us in becoming feminists have rejected the self-sacrificing, altruistic, infinitely

forgiving, martyred, unconditionally loving mother . . . have rejected that mother in *ourselves* as the part of ourselves which is complicitous in our own oppression.[14]

This may be why, as Sara Ruddick notes, so much women's writing is suffused with 'a nostalgia for a "paradise lost", an original mother-tongue, mother-home, mother-landscape that was sacrificed to the father's symbolic, Oedipal order'. It is not surprising, she says, that 'nostalgic fantasies for mothers or their bodies abound in feminist critiques of technocratic, patriarchal societies or that as *daughters*, mothers may participate in them'.[15]

This is not just a daughter's revolution, then, but a revolution of lost and abandoned and (to echo Adrienne Rich's much quoted phrase) 'wildly unmothered' daughters. So it is almost too neat a conceit that the much-discussed *Frankenstein* was written by Mary Shelley, the orphan whose mother, Mary Wollstonecraft, is also the mother of modern feminism. To go very quickly over this famous story – Mary Wollstonecraft died of puerperal fever two weeks after giving birth to the daughter we now know as Mary Shelley. The girl received a cold and lonely upbringing. Her father, William Godwin, seems to have been more interested in her education than in her company. Obsessed with her lost mother, Mary sought to be close to her by reading and rereading her mother's books and diaries, often while sitting on her mother's grave.[16] At sixteen she ran off to the Continent with the married and already known Percy Bysshe Shelley. During the years of travel that followed, she gave birth to two children, a daughter, born premature, who died at two weeks, and a son, who was to die aged three and a half. (Only one child, Percy, would make it into adulthood.) The woman who sat down in her cottage on the shores of Lac Leman to write *Frankenstein* was a woman steeped in the 'horror story of Maternity'.[17]

The idea for *Frankenstein* came to her after their neighbour, Lord Byron, suggested they all three write ghost stories. Hers came to her in the form of a waking dream. A nightmare, in which her worst fears about abandonment and its consequences found their true proportions. Like its author, every character in the novel is an orphan, but the cry of the abandoned child finds its most perfect, its most feminist, voice, in the confessions of the scientist Frankenstein's nameless creature.

His career in film has been largely speechless. As Boris Karloff so famously remarked, it was always a mistake to let Frankenstein's nameless creature speak. But the account the creature gives of his sorry existence is the heart of the original novel. Despite the fact that the creature is both man and monster, feminist scholars like Ellen Moers,[18] Sandra M. Gilbert and Susan Gubar[19] have argued that he is the character who best describes the world as the motherless young mother Mary Shelley then saw it.

The creature's creator, the scientist Frankenstein, was about as unmotherly as you can get. He abandoned his creature in horror as soon as it came to life, simply because it was too ugly to look at. It took a long time for the creature to work this one out. In the beginning, the creature claims, he was a gentle and impressionable soul with an infinite capacity for love. Ignorant of his origins, and puzzled by the horror he aroused in others, he wandered about the forest, eventually taking refuge outside a cottage inhabited by a blind, benevolent old man with an air of Milton about him, and his two fine grown-up children. The creature learned about family life by observing this family surreptitiously and slowly educated himself by borrowing his books. The one that made the greatest impression on him was Milton's own *Paradise Lost*. Although he read it as a 'true history' of creation, he was confused by it because it seemed to have no place for him:

> Like Adam, I was apparently united by no link to any other human in existence; but his state was different to mine. He had come forth from the hands of God a perfect creature, happy and prosperous, guarded by the especial care of his creator; he was allowed to converse with and acquire knowledge from beings of a superior nature: but I was wretched, helpless, and alone.[20]

> I was dependent on none, and related to none. The path of my departure was free, and there was none to lament my

annihilation. My person was hideous and my stature gigantic. What did this mean? Who was I? What was I? Whence did I come? What was my destination? These questions continually recurred, but I was unable to solve them.[21]

Until he found some papers in the pocket of the dress he had taken from the lab where he was created. These record the four months prior to his seeing the light of day:

. . . everything which bears reference to my accursed origin: the whole detail of that series of disgusting circumstances which produced it . . . the minutest description of my odious and loathsome person . . . in language which painted your own horrors, and rendered mine indelible. I sickened as I read. 'Hateful day when I received in agony.' Accursed creator! Why did you form a monster so hideous that even *you* turned from me in disgust? God, in pity, made man beautiful and alluring, after his own image, but my form is a filthy type of yours, more horrid even from the resemblance.[22]

Still he hoped that the cottagers, who were so kind to each other, would find it in their hearts to accept him. But the longer he thought about it, the more doubtful he became:

Increase of knowledge only discovered to me more clearly what a wretched outcast I was.
    I endeavoured to crush these fears and to fortify myself . . . sometimes I allowed thoughts, unchecked by reason, to ramble in the fields of Paradise, and dared to fancy amiable and lovely creatures sympathising with my feelings and cheering my gloom; their angelic countenances breathed smiles of consolation. But it was all a dream; no Eve soothed my sorrows nor shared my thoughts. I was alone. I remembered Adam's supplication to his creator. But where was mine? He had abandoned me and in the bitterness of my heart I cursed him.[23]

The cottagers still seemed to promise a reprieve. Seizing an opportunity to speak to the blind old man alone, the creature was interrupted by the sudden return of his children. The daughter was terrified by the creature's loathsome appearance and recoiled; the son met terror with violence. The creature recalls:

> I could have torn him limb from limb, as the lion rends the antelope. But my heart sank within me as with bitter sickness, and I refrained.[24]

This, say Gilbert and Gubar, is how Mary Shelley herself must have felt upon discovering that her father's society of learned men had no place for her, that the tradition to which he belonged did not even recognise her as fully human. This, they imply, is how all educated women feel at the moment when they discover that the cultural heritage that has shaped their minds has no place for them because of their bodies.[25]

This, I would go on to add, is how Mary Wollstonecraft felt upon reading Thomas Paine's *A Vindication of the Rights of Man*. This was the enraged insight that drove her to write her manifesto, *A Vindication of the Rights of Women*.

This, I would also go on to add, is the enraged insight – the betrayal – that gave birth to feminism. And that still feeds it to this day.

The bitterness of this betrayal is such that it blunts the obvious

That, for most of history, and in most places to this day, the society of learned men has excluded not just women, but most men, most colours, most classes, and most shades of opinion. But if it is comforting to know that we are keeping good company in our misery, this thought leads on to another which is a lot less comforting. We have all benefited from this wicked past: any democracy and diversity we enjoy today, we owe to millennia of injustices.

What can you do when your origins are corrupt? When the history that has made you, and that still determines what you see and how you behave, is even worse? These are not just feminist questions. But when they become feminist questions, the overriding desire is to deny the connection with these origins, and that history. To say, like Donna J. Haraway and the cyborg feminists, that these origins can be waived and forgotten. To imply, like so many others, that we had nothing to do with the making of that history. That men are the corrupt ones. That it's possible for women somehow to disown the legacy without having to disown themselves. But it's not possible. If you disown your legacy, you *do* disown yourself. Having disowned yourself, you grow to loathe any mirror that shows the family resemblances that have persisted anyway. Having committed yourself to making sure none of this evil genetic and cultural material gets passed on to yet another generation, you cannot help but see procreation as a dangerous, corrupt, and disgusting exercise, and all children resulting from it as potential monsters.

In this light, the strange prejudice against mothers is no longer an oversight or an accident. It is the central problem of modern feminism. It is the motor for the revolving-door logic of sexual politics. Feminist theory has a hard time with motherhood because it has a hard time with legacy, because it has a hard time acknowledging that it has benefited from this legacy, and that it reflects this legacy even when it doesn't want to, and perpetuates this legacy even as it is struggling to do the opposite. If you are unwilling to accept the cruel truths about the cultural heritage that has made you what you are, if you are unwilling to accept that, like it or not, the version you will be passing on to the next generation will, at best, be only slightly better, then you cannot help but think of mothers as corrupt beyond redemption. You cannot even look at a mother without seeing the ideological problem monstrously illustrated.

Look at me, for example. What have I done? Four times in a row, I've brought forth genetic aliens. I've had to accept them before I've had a chance even to see them. Having seen them, I still have no idea what they will become. No matter how hard and long I look into their faces, I'll never know which half of them is me and which half their father. No matter how hard I try, I'll never have full control over their upbringing. Rather, I'll be battling for influence, along with their fathers, teachers,

friends, books and favourite TV characters. I'll never manage to
be the mother I want to be, never get the right balance between
tradition and new ideas, home and work, them and me. I don't
know what kind of world I'll be sending them out into. Even if
I throw myself into it body and soul, the best I can hope for is
a mixed blessing. Even if I can't hope for more than that, I still
have to get up in the morning and do the best job I can. Survival
– mine and theirs – being always more urgent a question than
success or purity. I can see how anyone with time for reflection
might find this way of life unattractive, and seek an alternative.
But a room of one's own is not much of an alternative.

If you are supposed to be in the business of social transformation, a room of one's own is worse than a coward's refuge.
It is an unconditional surrender. One of the received wisdoms
that gets the most play in our inverted Gregorian chant is that
the logic of Western, and therefore man-made, civilization leads
to death. We are therefore meant to be the champions of life. I
cannot think of a single feminism that doesn't chant for life. The
New Age ideologues with their motherlines and the goddesses
within them chant for life. The radicals chant for life. And so do
the liberals, the Marxists, the psychoanalytics. Even the cyborg
feminists chant for life. This has been the mantra since Mary
Wollstonecraft: a world that makes room for liberated, better
educated, autonomous women will lead to a better world for
all of us. But for this better world to continue beyond our
generation, for it not to end in death, there needs to be a
generation after ours. If we can't conceive of a line going on
into the indefinite future, we can't conceive of hope and there
is no reason to struggle for faith. It makes no sense, then, that
the only lively line of resistance feminism has had to offer is the
denial of birth. Because if everybody denied birth, this strategy,
too, would lead to death. To extinction.

From time to time, authors who acknowledge this as the
logical conclusion of our prevailing stategy find the daring
to go so far as to point out that society would come to a
disastrous standstill overnight if the mothers of the world
all went simultaneously on strike. Whatever they say about
mothers in ivory towers and cabinet meetings, everyone knows
we are looking at the work that makes life, society, politics,

civilization, possible. If it is unlikely that the mothers of the world ever will go on strike, it's because we don't trust anyone else to do as good a job as we do. We value our work, even if we can't bring ourselves to say so in public. Even if we judge our performances harshly, we know we're indispensable.

So why has there been a reluctance inside feminist theory to look at childrearing as anything but a trap? It's not just because it's an 'extra' responsibility that puts you at an unnecessary disadvantage. It's also because it involves co-operating and negotiating with people and institutions the movement would prefer to avoid. Because it involves responsibilities and nagging questions and the half-hearted collusions that responsibilities always drag along behind them. It's easier for our great thinkers to go into the type of denial we like to think of as male, to pretend mothering is dull work best left to lesser beings who don't mind putting themselves last. And (like the men they are pretending to differ from) they are content to preside over us blindly and from a great distance with pious censure.

But where does this tactic leave us? Yes, who *is* going to look after the children? When Betty Friedan asked this question she assumed, with the benevolent arrogance of the experienced mother, that we always know how. But you have only to open a newspaper to realise that most parties in this discussion haven't a clue. People talk about childcare packages and flexible schedules as if that was all there was to it.

How to explain to these people the vastness and the complexity of our invisible world? How to let these people in without their trampling all over our invisible values? The very idea fills me with horror, a horror I see reflected in *Frankenstein*, which contains the mother's view of children as well as a daughter's view of creation. You will remember that it wasn't the scientist Frankenstein's Faustian arrogance that turned his creature from a freak into a monster bent on death and destruction. It was not just his creator's rejection and abandonment of him. Nor was it his expulsion from the same brotherhood of learned men whose books had shaped his understanding. No, it was his creator's later refusal to make a mate for him, this man's ignorance of the redemptive possibilities of kindness, and his decision to deny the monster both the society of his own kind, as well as the chance to create children and a future in their joint image. These are the traditional responsibilities of the mother, to turn children, no matter how monstrous they may appear, into fully fledged members of the human race. To keep enough faith in the people they could become so that it is possible for them to become these people. To bring them up so that they are, in one way or another, part of the story. Being part of the story may or may not involve having children. What it does almost always mean is seeing what you do in terms of maintaining life.

So the question I have about feminism is: *Does* it continue life? Or is it still in the throes of the original betrayal that gave rise to it? Still afraid to grow up? Still in thrall to the mothers who sold us short? Still trying to figure out how to grow up without having to risk getting or causing damage? Still stuck?

And if it is stuck, then what about us?

This is *our* legacy, too. What are we going to do about it?

9

YES, WHAT *ABOUT* US?

Can we save this movement, or is it going to sink out of sight again for another few generations?

In *A Room of One's Own*, Virginia Woolf suggested that female tradition was different from male tradition because women thought back through their mothers.[1] This confident, practical understanding of genetic and domestic continuity finds little echo in the history of feminism. Generation does not follow on effortlessly from generation. There are gaps, reactions, unexplained silences, deaf ears, and lost legacies.

An example: Mary Wollstonecraft asserted the rights of women, and tried to live by her egalitarian ideas, but then the campaigners who took over from her did not want her mantle, because she was too racy, she had once been an unwed mother, she would weaken their claim to be respectable women worthy of the vote. This pattern of repudiations has repeated itself many times over. Each time it happens, the disagreement hinges on motherhood.

One of the many myths that gave rise to second-wave feminism is that the first wave peaked when women got the vote in the twenties, enjoyed a faint revival during the war years when women had to work for the war effort, and then died absolutely until the first sixties housewife marched out into the suburban sunset. The real story, of course, is more complicated. Actually, there were respectable numbers of women in the professions all through the thirties, with professional organisations to offer proper support. If they failed to inspire the younger masses, it was partly because of their killjoy reputations. It was because the thing they called emancipation looked so much like duty, repression, virginal silence, and in other words, perpetual daughterhood. Perpetual obedient daughterhood. These ageing suffragettes seemed motherly in the worst sense of the word, while modern women wanted to be themselves, enjoy some freedom of movement, be outrageous, have fun.

So they turned away from the tweed skirts and the sensible brown shoes and looked instead to the glamorous women in the news. In the twenties and thirties women were especially prominent in the industries that were still in their infancy. Aviation brought us Amelia Earhart. Hollywood gave us Mae West, Katharine Hepburn, Bette Davis. In the arts there were Georgia O'Keeffe, Martha Graham and Dorothy Parker. These women were famous for their ability to combine excellence and daring with an intelligent brand of femininity.[2]

The war is one reason these icons went out of style – to make room for other, more troop-friendly models. Another reason is that those glamorous role models seldom had children. This is the common bond between the icons and those more earnest, politically minded women who worked so hard to break down old barriers in their professions. They tended not to have children either.[3]

For many of them, not having children was an ideological decision. The lines of battle inside feminism were clear in those days. If you supported equal rights, you were fighting for the right to be treated like a man, and therefore under some obligation not to act like a woman. If you supported protective legislation for women because they had this habit of becoming mothers, and this knack of accumulating families, then the idea of equal rights was anathema. The US feminist movement fell apart during the thirties because these two wings of feminism were unable to resolve their differences. In the UK, the same and just as bitter dispute ended any hope of feminist co-operation across class boundaries. Working-class women in the Labour Party supported protective legislation: they bitterly resented non-party middle-class feminists (rich, idle ladies, they called them) who continued to support the principle of equal rights even at a time when it would cost working-class women dearly. The split cost women in the Labour Party dearly, too. As they severed their remaining links with the feminist movement,

no!

and sought instead to blend into class struggle with their male colleagues, they dropped out of sight. By the thirties there was not a single Labour woman at the national level.[4]

The pro-family lobby today is a thing of the right. This has cost the women's movement more than just a few supporters. The classic reason why a non-middle-class woman in this country will not call herself a feminist is the same as it was in the thirties – because she prefers to call herself a wife or mother. Even so, the equity–equality dispute persists in feminism today. It comes in many polite disguises, but if you take them apart you will always find that the real split, the question that cannot ever be allowed to be seen naked, is this question about motherhood. Is it something to be cherished, or something to escape? Something women want because they are women, or something they want because they've been brainwashed? If you help women who want to be mothers, are you making it harder for other women to pursue any other course? Are you perpetuating patriarchy? Killing any hope of gender equality? Even if you are in favour of motherhood, or at least of having children, how do you proceed, how do you manage to do it your way, how do you free yourself from the shadow of your own mother? How do you find out what traditions you want to keep and what traditions you want to alter? How do you find out what your mother thinks? How do you break the taboo of silence? How do you create a spoken, public continuity between mother and daughter? What do you make of the same problems when they break the continuity of the feminist movement itself?

These are the unasked questions that have created the rifts inside feminism from the very beginning, that have kept one generation from building upon the work of the generation that preceded it, and that threaten its future even today. It is as difficult for feminists to accept feminist legacy as it is for feminists to accept the so-called patriarchal legacy. It's difficult because feminism is not for mothers, but for daughters. Daughters who don't want to listen to the mothers they can't talk back to. Daughters who don't want to become mothers, who can't see eye to eye with their sisters who do. Daughters who don't become mothers get a hell of a lot more done in the world than their sisters who become mothers, but because they have no daughters of their own, because they can't co-operate with their sisters who do, they are, in the end, unable to pass on the benefits of their hard-won victories. And so herstory gets lost, and forgotten, and repeated. Generation after generation, the only woman who gets into history is the honourable exception. The story of what all the other women have got up to remains off the record.

Does it have to go on like this? I think there is a way out of the trap. We could start by looking at this prejudice against mothers, and take it apart, try to understand it. I mean all of us. We need to break the silence. Stop confining our understanding of politics to body politics. Stop ignoring what women actually do. Start helping them do it. Make feminism more than entertainment again. Take the initiative not just on behalf of women but on behalf of the people who depend on them. This would involve leaving behind the obsessions of sexual politics, and the paraphernalia of betrayal – the fall from grace, the cry of abandonment, the never ending Oedipal vendetta, the woman's body as site of oppression, the patriarch as invisible freemason, the mother who must be content to remain powerless in life because she is so powerful in symbol. It would involve looking very carefully at class and race prejudices about mothers, and the history of class and race prejudices against mothers inside feminism.

It would mean understanding and clarifying the issues of maternal practice by actually listening to and encouraging debate – and that means not just amongst women of all classes and races and religions but also men. It would involve moving beyond the clumsy talk of nurseries and day care and maternal leave and quarrels over what fathers can and cannot do, and looking at the larger picture, at what children need from their parents, and what parents need for themselves and for their children, at patterns of paid work and unpaid work, as they exist now, and as they could become if things were arranged in such a way that all people who worked for pay had enough time left over for their unpaid responsibilities.

I don't see the outcome as feminist, but I think that, unless feminists are the catalysts, and unless feminism embraces the viewpoint of mothers, it's not going to happen. Simply because we are talking about a maternal tradition that we know more about, and that continues to be our responsibility if only because we feel obliged, as mothers, to protect the weak against everyone's else's indifference. And here again, I mean all feminists, the equity ones and the equality ones, the ones who would rather die than become their mothers, as well as the ones who are mothers.

I think it's theoretically possible to resolve the equality–equity problem by ceasing to consider it solely in relation to women. Instead of saying that all women deserve equal rights with men, or all women deserve protective legislation because they have children, you need to broaden things out a little. You say all men and women have the same rights under the law, and all men and women need certain protections because they have families. You say it is wrong for anyone, male or female, to have to become an economic dependant in order to bring up children. It is wrong to penalise those who are bringing up children with second-class citizenship. You say, also, it is very hard to bring children up alone, or even inside a two-parent family, and that all parents, whether or not they're married or single, or male or female, need various forms of social support. You say all these things, and then you legislate accordingly. At least in theory.

In practice, I say all these things and I'm talking to the wall. Which is, because it's all in one piece and one place, a near perfect conversationalist in comparison to the women's movement that changed my life and then went headless and disembodied with, as Kate Figes has pointed out, no forwarding address.

There are feminists, feminists everywhere, but no two who can agree. And mothers, mothers everywhere, who are too tied down to change the world on their own. As well as fathers who are not just marginalised at work if they take parenting seriously, but marginalised inside the society of mothers and almost invisible inside what passes for feminist debate.

We are too divided to help each other, and we have few outside allies. The people who have the time and the clout to help us, the feminists who have said no to the double load, are too angry, too consumed with the indignity they suffered from some sexist somewhere yesterday, too likely to turn the page the moment they see the dread word 'mother'. Too happy in those rooms of their own, too busy redefining their sexuality, having too much fun in their postmodern integrated circuits. While those of us who are bringing up families today are too stretched, too discouraged, too weighed down with our double *un'l then?* loads even to dream of a way to attract their attention. When I think of the effort it would take to get the broad support we need to work collectively to tackle these problems I see so clearly, my first thought is: How am I ever going to get them to listen? My second thought is: Where would I find the energy to go on and on and on to an audience of deaf ears? My third thought is to go to bed.

A bed of one's own. Is that what it's come to?

Another nightmare

When I was a child living in Istanbul, there was a house we sometimes passed on our way to school. It was on the longer, scenic route that my father preferred and sometimes insisted on, especially – or so it seemed – when we were already late. So it was usually in a doomed and dreading state of mind that I passed this house, which was larger than its neighbours, had an unusual amount of dark-red patterned brickwork, and an appearance that I would now call Gothic.

On the second or third floor there was a grand panelled door. It may or may not have been oak but the word 'oak' is at least faithful to the impression it created. But the most striking thing about the door was that it led nowhere.

Why? I used to wonder. Had there been a staircase once upon a time? A terrace? A balcony? If so, it had left no trace. The door was a mockery of its architect's presumed intentions. In my nightmares, it was even worse – an invitation to walk on air and take the consequences. In my nightmares, I was always inside this house looking out. Usually there was something horrible going on that I was desperate to escape from. Seeing the mock door, I would throw it open, and then, embracing the beautiful sunny day or the moonlit night and the always vast view of the Bosporus and its Asian shore, I would put my best foot forward only to find – sometimes just in time and sometimes not – that there was nothing for me to stand on.

That's what the feminist future looks like from my vantage point. A grand doorway affording any number of grand views, inviting me to step out but leading into thin air.

How to connect the door to the view, the badly designed present to the prizewinning future? How to bring up children in the meantime? How to make sure we have more to pass on to them than a gaping hole, an empty promise, and a view? How to get that staircase done before they want to leave? Who are we building it with, anyway – the men inside who won't listen? The men outside who don't want to know? The women making mud pies below us and Utopias on the horizon?

And what about us? How many of us are there, and how much are we willing to put ourselves on the line? How the hell do I know? Here I am spouting the word 'collective action', but I don't have a clue how collective action happens.

Maybe once upon a time I believed that Change was Possible when hundreds of thousands of people simultaneously and spontaneously reached the same righteous conclusion. And that, when they all went outside and screamed with one voice, the politicians took notice. Now I know better. For the last sixteen years, I've watched working parents whisper their betrayed conclusions to each other and then go inside and scream alone. We have done next to nothing as a group to ease the strains. Forget an integrated childcare policy – we haven't even asked for the simplest reform of all – which is to redesign school hours so that they mesh with work hours.

If you even mention the words integrated childcare policy, people shrug their shoulders, and someone inevitably says oh, wouldn't that be nice, but it will never happen, because it would cost too much money. But that can't be right. It couldn't possibly cost as much to an economy as a workforce that has to come close to killing itself just to cope. And anyway, the problem is not money, but the organisation of work. And the organisation of the work day – in other words, time.

X You know what I'd like? I'd like to be able to do my jobs X well. That's all! That's not very revolutionary, now is it? In fact, it's so unrevolutionary, I'm almost embarrassed to admit it. Even so, I've set my sights too high. I don't stand a chance of doing my jobs well, because there aren't enough hours in the day. There would be enough hours in the day if the work day and the domestic day were changed. And they wouldn't even have to be changed that much. But that would involve everyone making changes in their schedules, not just parents, and in the present climate, what likelihood is there of that?

Not to worry, heavy-lidded sages tell me. It's early days yet. You've done your best. Your values will be reflected in your children's attitudes. Everything will work out eventually. In a generation or two, or three at the outside, we'll have all the details worked out. Thanks to your thankless struggles, your grandchildren will have better lives. Better to accept your lot, they say – because fighting your lot only makes life hard and bitter. In the meantime, one must keep one's sense of perspective. To enlarge upon Scarlett O'Hara, tomorrow is another century.

But this is just not good enough

I'm tired of being fobbed off with the long view. It's too much like being fobbed off with a promise of an afterlife. Ideas don't just happen. If you want them to prevail, you've still got to fight for them. You still have to make yourself heard, even if it's not the right climate. And if you're trying to engage with people who don't want to listen, you've got to make them listen. You've got to force them to acknowledge that there is a gap between the life they think you lead and the life you do live, the symbol they see and the woman you are. This is not a departure from feminism, but a completion of the original idea.

Once upon a time I was just a girl who had no idea where her own thoughts ended and the eye of the beholder began. Into this confusion came a crude protofeminist idea – that anyone who did not see me the way I wanted to be seen was treating me like an Object. What I saw or what I intended is anyone's guess – my photographs of the time show a teenager wavering uncertainly and unoriginally between hot pants with platform shoes and jeans with red bandanas. I can only imagine what a ridiculous figure I must have cut on the many occasions when I accused suspected chauvinists of treating me like a sex object – but better to have had this defence and this formula than nothing at all. Because the idea that there might be a difference between what I intended and what other people saw led to questions like: What *do* I intend? What do I see that they don't see? Who am I? Where am I going? Why? These are the questions without which no degree of autonomy is possible, and these are the questions that cannot happen if you are marooned inside the eye of the beholder. If I've been able to ask them and move on from them, it's thanks to feminism. This is the debt that I'll never be able to repay.

The problem is that the ideas behind this project have never been properly extended to motherhood. Step into this so-called rut and you walk into a no man's land that makes your previous life as a sex object look almost desirable. At least when you're a sex object you get noticed, and sought after, and fought over. When you become a Mother Object people only notice you when they need you to do something or when you have dared to depart from their ideas about what mothers ought to do. It's no accident, I think, that, in more than half of the family photos in which I've appeared since having children, I've featured as a pair of arms holding a birthday cake.

Well, I'm tired of being a Mother Object. Tired of being the invisible workhorse, tired of providing the blank screen for everyone else's archetypes and the playground for their contradictions. Life is hard enough without this crap! Time to put a stop to it. Time to set these people straight. Time to disown the mask. Time to ask for something better. Time to insist on life after childbirth. Full lives, with all rights reserved.

I can't imagine that agitation along these lines will lead

214

instantly to a brilliant exposition of life as we know it and as we want it to become, and the political changes we need. But it does open up the hope that it might one day become possible. And it's a hell of a lot better than betrayed, frozen, stoical silence.

That's what I think, anyway. What about you?

NOTES

I

1. Didion, Joan, 'The Women's Movement', *The White Album* (Penguin London, 1986) p.110
2. Greer, Germaine, *The Female Eunuch* (Flamingo London, 1993) p.361
3. Ibid., p.366
4. Ibid., p.369
5. Ibid., p.370
6. Ibid.
7. Millett, Kate, *Sexual Politics* (Virago London, 1991) p.xi
8. Wollstonecraft, Mary, *A Vindication of the Rights of Women* (Penguin London, 1992) p.304
9. Ibid.
10. de Beauvoir, Simone, *The Second Sex* (Bantam New York, 1970) p.484
11. Ibid., p.467
12. Friedan, Betty, *The Feminine Mystique* (Penguin London, 1992) p.289
13. Ibid., p.228
14. Ibid., p.244
15. Greer, Germaine, *The Female Eunuch* (Flamingo London, 1993) p.74
16. Ibid., p.81
17. Ibid.
18. Ibid., p.87
19. Ibid., p.263
20. Ibid., p.264
21. Badinter, Elisabeth, *Man/Woman: The One is the Other* (Collins Harvill London, 1989)
22. Friedan, Betty, *The Second Stage* (Abacus London, 1981) p.331
23. Chodorow, Nancy, *The Reproduction of Mothering: Psychoanalysis and the Sociology of Gender* (University of California Press Berkeley, 1978)
24. Benhabib, Seyla and Cornell, Drucilla, *Feminism as Critique* (Polity/ Blackwell Cambridge Oxford, 1987)
25. Faludi, Susan, *Backlash: The Undeclared War Against Women* (Chatto London, 1991) p.350
26. Wolf, Naomi, *Fire with Fire: The New Female Power and How It Will Change the 21st Century* (Chatto London, 1993) pp.275–304
27. Ibid., pp.140–143
28. Roiphe, Katie, *The Morning After: Sex, Fear and Feminism on Campus* (Hamish Hamilton London, 1993) p.174
29. Ibid., p.16

NOTES

30. Ibid., p.85
31. Ibid., pp.138–60
32. Paglia, Camille, *Sex, Art and American Culture* (Viking London, 1992) p.89
33. Ibid.
34. Ibid., p.90
35. Ibid., pp.22–4
36. Haraway, Donna J., *Simians, Cyborgs and Women: The Reinvention of Nature* (Free Association Books London, 1994) Preface
37. Velmans, Marianne and Litvinoff, Sarah, *Working Mother: A Practical Handbook for the Nineties* (Pocket Books New York, 1993) p.393
38. Ibid.
39. Estes, Clarissa Pinkola, *Women Who Run with the Wolves* (Rider Books London, 1993) p.39
40. Crosby, Faye J., *Juggling* (Macmillan New York, 1993) p.197
41. Ibid., p.198
42. Ibid., p.156
43. Ibid.

II

1. Spelman, Elizabeth V., *Inessential Woman* (The Women's Press London, 1988)
2. hooks, bell, *Feminist Theory: From Margin to Center* (South End Press Boston, 1984) pp.133–4
3. Martin, Emily, *The Woman in the Body* (Open University Press Buckingham, 1989) (attributed to Berger and Luckman) p.11
4. O'Brien, Mary, *The Politics of Reproduction* (Routledge London, 1981) p.8
5. Elshtain, Jean Bethke, *Public Man/Private Woman: Women in Social and Political Thought* (Princeton University Press Princeton, 1981)
6. Ibid.
7. Ruddick, Sara, *Maternal Thinking: Towards a Politics of Peace* (The Women's Press London, 1989) p.28
8. Ibid.

III

1. Dinnerstein, Dorothy, *The Mermaid and the Minotaur: Sexual Arrangements and Human Malaise* (Harper Colophon Books New York, 1977) pp.5–6
2. Ibid., p.7
3. Ibid.
4. Ibid., p.259
5. Ibid., p.260
6. Ibid., p.265
7. Ibid., p.264
8. Ibid., p.266
9. Ibid., p.266
10. Ibid., pp.266–7

11. Ibid., pp.267–8
12. Ibid., p.273
13. Ibid., pp.273–5
14. Ibid., p.277
15. Chodorow, Nancy, *The Reproduction of Mothering: Psychoanalysis and the Sociology of Gender* (University of California Press Berkeley, 1978) pp.218–19
16. Rich, Adrienne, *Of Woman Born: Motherhood as Experience and Institution* (Virago London, 1977) p.6
17. Ibid., p.21
18. Ibid., p.27
19. Ibid.
20. Ibid., p.195
21. Ibid., p.277
22. Ibid., p.222
23. Ibid., p.225
24. In *The Reproduction of Mothering* Nancy Chodorow suggests that it is an incest taboo that has left this story untold. If incest taboos exist to help perpetuate the species, then it follows that the incest scenario that would end the human race, and that therefore must be suppressed at all costs, would be the one in which all childless daughters fall in love with their mothers
25. Rich, Adrienne, *Of Woman Born: Motherhood as Experience and Institution*, p.225
26. Ibid., p.211
27. Ibid., p.224
28. Ibid., p.252
29. de Beauvoir, Simone, *The Second Sex* (Bantam New York, 1970) p.466
30. Ibid., p.467
31. Ibid., p.468
32. Ibid.
33. Rich, Adrienne, *Of Woman Born: Motherhood as Experience and Institution*, p.40
34. de Beauvoir, Simone, *The Second Sex*, p.252
35. Rich, Adrienne, *Of Woman Born: Motherhood as Experience and Institution*, p.68
36. Ibid., p.55
37. Ibid., p.39
38. Ibid., p.284
39. Ibid.
40. Ibid.

VII

1. Coward, Rosalind, *Our Treacherous Hearts: Why We Let Men Have Their Way* (Faber London, 1993) p.105
2. Ibid.
3. Ibid., p.106
4. Ibid., p.117
5. Ibid., p.10
6. Elson, Diane, 'Unpaid Labour, Macroeconomic Adjustment and Macroeconomic Strategies', Working Paper for Gender Analysis and Development Economics (University of Manchester Manchester, 1993) p.3

7. Evans, A. and Young, K., 'Gender Issues in Household Labour Allocation in the Case of Northern Province, Zambia', ESCOR Report (Overseas Development Administration London, 1988)
8. Elson, Diane, 'Unpaid Labour, Macroeconomic Adjustment and Macro-economic Strategies', p.4
9. Ibid., p.6
10. Moser, C., 'The Impact of the Recession and Structural Adjustment Policies at the Micro Level: Low-income Women and their Households in Guayaquil, Ecuador', *Invisible Adjustment*, Vol. 2 (UNICEF New York, 1989)
11. Elson, Diane, 'Unpaid Labour, Macroeconomic Adjustment and Macro-economic Strategies', p.7
12. Ibid.
13. Ibid., p.10
14. Figes, Kate, *Because of Her Sex: The Myth of Equality for Women in Britain* (Macmillan London, 1994) pp.129–30
15. Ibid., pp.132–3
16. Ibid., p.133
17. Ibid., p.104
18. Swiss, Deborah J. and Walker, Judith P., *Women and the Work/Family Dilemma: How Today's Professional Women are Finding Solutions* (John Wiley and Sons New York, 1993) pp.10–11
19. Ibid., p.1
20. Ibid., p.5
21. Hochschild, Dr Arlie, *The Second Shift: Working Parents and the Revolution at Home* (Piatkus London, 1989) p.256
22. Swiss, Deborah J. and Walker, Judith P., *Women and the Work/Family Dilemma: How Today's Professional Women are Finding Solutions*, p.219
23. Ibid., p.224

VIII

1. Spelman, Elizabeth V., *Inessential Woman* (The Women's Press London, 1988)
2. O'Brien, Mary, *The Politics of Reproduction* (Routledge London, 1981)
3. Kristeva, Julia, 'Stabat Mater', *The Kristeva Reader* (Blackwell Oxford, 1986) p.179
4. Ruddick, Sara, *Maternal Thinking: Towards a Politics of Peace* (The Women's Press London, 1989)
5. Elshtain, Jean Bethke, *Public Man/Private Woman: Women in Social and Political Thought* (Princeton University Press Princeton, 1981) p.337
6. Ibid.
7. Everingham, Christine, *Mothers and Maternity* (Open University Press Buckingham, 1994)
8. Ellmann, Mary, *Thinking About Women* (Virago London 1979) pp.2–3
9. Haste, Helen, *The Sexual Metaphor* (Harvester Wheatsheaf Hemel Hempstead 1993)
10. Segal, Lynne, *Straight Sex: The Politics of Pleasure* (Virago London, 1994)
11. Hillman, James, 'On Betrayal', *Loose Ends* (Spring Publications Dallas Texas, 1975

12. Ruddick, Sara, *Maternal Thinking: Towards a Politics of Peace*, p.34, ref.5

13. Kristeva, Julia, 'Stabat Mater', p.164

14. Ruddick Sara, *Maternal Thinking: Towards a Politics of Peace*, pp.38–9, ref.12

15. Ibid., p.38

16. Gilbert, Sandra M. and Gubar, Susan, *The Madwoman in the Attic: The Woman Writer and the Nineteenth-century Literary Imagination* (Yale University Press New Haven, 1979), p.223

17. Ibid., p.299

18. Moers, Ellen, *Literary Women* (Doubleday New York, 1976)

19. Gilbert, Sandra M. and Gubar, Susan, *The Madwoman in the Attic: The Woman Writer and the Nineteenth-century Literary Imagination*

20. Shelley, Mary, *Frankinstein* (Penguin London, 1992) p.126

21. Ibid., p.124

22. Ibid., p.126

23. Ibid., p.127

24. Ibid., pp.127–8

25. Gilbert, Sandra M. and Gubar, Susan, *The Madwoman in the Attic: The Woman Writer and the Nineteenth-century Literary Imagination*

IX

1. Woolf, Virginia, *A Room of One's Own* (Harcourt Brace and World New York, 1929) p.79

2. Ware, Susan, *Still Missing: Amelia Earhart and the Search for Modern Feminism* (W. W. Norton New York/London, 1993)

3. See also Cott, Nancy, *The Grounding of Modern Feminism* (Yale University Press New Haven, 1987)

4. Graves, Pamela M., *Labour Women: Women in British Working-Class Politics, 1918–1939* (Cambridge University Press Cambridge, 1994)

BIBLIOGRAPHY

Archer, John and Lloyd, Barbara, *Sex and Gender* (Penguin London, 1982)

Badinter, Elisabeth, *Man/Woman: The One is the Other* (Collins Harvill London, 1989)

Barrett, Michele and McIntosh, Mary, *The Antisocial Family* (Verso London, 1982)

Benhabib, Seyla and Cornell, Drucilla, Benhabib S., 'The General and the Concrete Other' and Markus, Maria, 'Women, Success and Civil Society', *Feminism as Critique* (Polity/Blackwell Cambridge Oxford, 1987)

Benjamin, Jessica, *The Bonds of Love* (Virago London, 1990)

Billington, Rachel, *The Great Umbilical* (Hutchinson London, 1994)

Brown, Norman O., *Life Against Death: The Psychoanalytic Meaning of History* (Vintage New York, 1959)

Butler, Judith, *Bodies That Matter* (Routledge London, 1993)

Chodorow, Nancy, *The Reproduction of Mothering: Psychoanalysis and the Sociology of Gender* (University of California Press Berkeley, 1978)

Corea, Gena, *The Mother Machine* (The Women's Press London, 1985)

Cott, Nancy, *The Grounding of Modern Feminism* (Yale University Press New Haven, 1987)

Coward, Rosalind, *Our Treacherous Hearts: Why We Let Men Have Their Way* (Faber London, 1993)

Crosby, Faye J., *Juggling* (Macmillan New York, 1993)

Dally, Ann, *Inventing Motherhood: The Consequences of an Ideal* (Burnett London, 1982)

de Beauvoir, Simone, *The Second Sex* (Bantam New York, 1970)

Dench, Geoff, *The Frog Prince and the Problem of Men* (Neanderthal Books London, 1994)

Didion, Joan, *The White Album* (Penguin London, 1986)

Dinnerstein, Dorothy, *The Mermaid and the Minotaur: Sexual Arrangements and Human Malaise* (Harper Colophon Books New York, 1977)

Ehrenreich, Barbara and English, Deirdre, *For Her Own Good: Fifty Years of the Experts' Advice to Women* (Anchor Press New York, 1978)

Elliot, Faith Robertson, *The Family: Change or Continuity?* (Macmillan London, 1988)

Ellmann, Mary, *Thinking About Women* (Virago London, 1979)

Elshtain, Jean Bethke, *Public Man/Private Woman: Women in Social and Political Thought* (Princeton University Press Princeton, 1981)

Elson, Diane, 'Unpaid Labour, Macroeconomic Adjustment and Macroeconomic Strategies', Working Paper for Gender Analysis and Development Economics (University of Manchester Manchester, 1993)

Engels, Frederick, *The Origin of the Family, Private Property and the State* (International Publishers New York, 1968)

Estes, Clarissa Pinkola, *Women Who Run with the Wolves* (Rider Books London, 1993)

Evans, A., and Young, K., 'Gender Issues in Household Labour Allocation: the Case of Northern Province, Zambia', ESCOR Report (Overseas Development Administration London, 1988)

Everingham, Christine, *Motherhood and Modernity* (Open University Press Buckingham, 1994)

Faludi, Susan, *Backlash: The Undeclared War Against Women* (Chatto London, 1991)

Figes, Eva, *Patriarchal Attitudes* (Virago London, 1978)

Figes, Kate, *Because of Her Sex: The Myth of Equality for Women Today* (Macmillan London, 1994)

Firestone, Shulamith, *The Dialectic of Sex: The Case for Feminist Revolution* (The Women's Press London, 1979)

Fisher, Helen E., *The Sex Contract* (Paladin London, 1982)

French, Marilyn, *The War Against Women* (Hamish Hamilton London, 1992)

Friday, Nancy, *My Mother My Self* (Fontana London, 1979)

Friedan, Betty, *The Second Stage* (Abacus London, 1981)

Friedan, Betty, *The Feminine Mystique* (Penguin London, 1992)

Gilbert, Harriet, ed., *The Sexual Imagination* (Cape London, 1993)

Gilbert, Sandra M. and Gubar, Susan, *The Madwoman in the Attic: The Woman Writer and the Nineteenth-century Imagination* (Yale University Press New Haven, 1979)

Gilligan, Carol, *In a Different Voice: Psychological Theory and Women's Development* (Harvard University Press Cambridge, Massachusetts, 1993)

Gilman, Charlotte Perkins, *Herland* (The Women's Press London, 1979)

Grant, Linda, *Sexing the Millennium* (HarperCollins London, 1994)

Graves, Pamela M., *Labour Women: Women in British Working-class Politics, 1918–1939* (Cambridge University Press Cambridge, 1994)

Greer, Germaine, *The Female Eunuch* (Flamingo London, 1993)

Haraway, Donna J., *Simians, Cyborgs and Women: The Reinvention of Nature* (Free Association Books London, 1994)

Hardyment, Christina, *Dream Babies* (Oxford University Press Oxford 1993)

Haste, Helen, *The Sexual Metaphor* (Harvester Wheatsheaf Hemel Hempstead, 1993)

Hillman, James, 'On Betrayal', *Loose Ends* (Spring Publications Dallas Texas, 1975)

Hite, Shere, *Women and Love: A Cultural Revolution in Progress* (Penguin London, 1987)

Hochschild, Dr Arlie, *The Second Shift: Working Parents and the Revolution at Home* (Piatkus London, 1989)

hooks, bell, *Feminist Theory: From Margin to Center* (South End Press Boston, 1984)

Jackson, Deborah, *Do Not Disturb* (Bloomsbury London, 1993)

Kaplan, Cora, *Sea Changes: Culture and Feminism* (Verso London, 1986)

Kristeva, Julia, ed. Toril Moi, *The Kristeva Reader* (Blackwell Oxford, 1986)

Lowinsky, Naomi Ruth, *The Motherline: Every Woman's Journey to Find Her Female Roots* (Jeremy P. Tarcher Perigree Books New York, 1992)

BIBLIOGRAPHY

McConville, Brigid, *Mad to Be a Mother: Is There Life After Birth for Women Today?* (Century London, 1987)

MacKinnon, Catharine, *Feminism Unmodified* (Harvard University Press Cambridge, Massachusetts, 1987)

MacKinnon, Catharine, *Only Words* (HarperCollins London, 1994)

Malthus, Thomas, *An Essay on Population* (Dent London, 1958)

Martin, Emily, *The Woman in the Body* (Open University Press Buckingham, 1989)

Millett, Kate, *Sexual Politics* (Virago London, 1991)

Mitchell, Juliet, *Psychoanalysis and Feminism* (Penguin London, 1982)

Moers, Ellen, *Literary Women* (Doubleday New York, 1976)

Moi, Toril, *French Feminist Thought: A Reader* (Blackwell Oxford, 1987)

Moser, C., 'The Impact of Recession and Structural Adjustment Policies at the Micro Level: Low-income Women and their Households in Guayaquil, Ecuador', *Invisible Adjustment*, Vol. 2 (UNICEF New York, 1989)

Neustatter, Angela, *Hyenas in Petticoats* (Harrap London, 1989)

O'Brien, Mary, *The Politics of Reproduction* (Routledge London, 1981)

Oakley, Ann, *Becoming a Mother* (Martin Robertson Oxford, 1979)

Oakley, Ann *Subject Women* (Fontana London, 1983)

Olivier, Christiane, *Jocasta's Children: The Imprint of the Mother* (Routledge London, 1989)

Paglia, Camille, *Sex, Art and American Culture* (Viking London, 1992)

Rabuzzi, *Mother With Child: Transformations Through Childbirth* (Indiana University Press Bloomington, 1994)

Ribbens, Jane, *Mothers and Their Children* (Sage, 1994)

Rich, Adrienne, *Of Woman Born: Motherhood as Experience and Institution* (Virago London, 1977)

Richard, Janet Radcliffe, *The Sceptical Feminist* (Penguin London, 1980)

Roiphe, Katie, *The Morning After: Sex, Fear and Feminism on Campus* (Hamish Hamilton, 1993)

Rose, Phyllis, *Parallel Lives: Five Victorian Marriages* (Chatto London, 1984)

Ruddick, Sara, *Maternal Thinking: Towards a Politics of Peace* (The Women's Press London, 1989)

Sayers, Janet, *Mothering and Psychoanalysis* (Penguin London, 1991)

Scott, Joan W., 'Deconstructing Equality-Versus Difference: or *The Uses of Poststructuralist Theory for Feminism* (Feminist Studies 14 no. 1, Spring 1988)

Segal, Lynne, ed., *What Is to Be Done About the Family?* (Penguin London, 1983)

Segal, Lynne, *Is the Future Female?: Troubled Thoughts on Contemporary Feminism* (Virago London, 1987)

Segal, Lynne, *Slow Motion: Changing Masculinities Changing Men* (Virago London, 1990)

Segal, Lynne, *Straight Sex: The Politics of Pleasure* (Virago London, 1994)

Shelley, Mary, *Frankenstein* (Penguin, 1992)

Spelman, Elizabeth V., *Inessential Woman* (The Women's Press London, 1988)

Spender, Dale, ed., *Feminist Theorists* (The Women's Press London, 1992)

Steinem, Gloria, *Revolution From Within* (Corgi London, 1993)

Swiss, Deborah J. and Walker, Judith P., *Women and the Work/Family Dilemma: How Today's Professional Women are Finding Solutions* (John Wiley and Sons New York, 1993)

Tannen, Deborah, *You Just Don't Understand* (Virago London, 1991)

Velmans, Marianne and Litvinoff, Sarah, *Working Mother: A Practical Handbook for the Nineties* (Pocket Books New York, 1993)

Ware, Susan, *Still Missing: Amelia Earhart and the Search for Modern Feminism* (W. W. Norton New York/London, 1993)

Wilson, Elizabeth, *Hidden Agendas: Theory, Politics and Experience in the Women's Movement* (Tavistock London, 1986)

Wolf, Naomi, *The Beauty Myth* (Vintage London, 1990)

Wolf, Naomi, *Fire with Fire: The New Female Power and How It Will Change the 21st Century* (Chatto London, 1993)

Wollstonecraft, Mary, *A Vindication of the Rights of Women* (Penguin London, 1992)

Woolf, Virginia, *A Room of One's Own* (Harcourt Brace and World New York, 1929)

A Note on the Author

Maureen Freely writes regularly on women's issues for the *Independent on Sunday*, the *Observer* and the *Guardian*. She is also the author of four novels, *Mother's Helper, The Stork Club, The Life of the Party* and *Under the Vulcania*, and of a non-fiction work on fertility choices, *Pandora's Clock*, which she co-authored with Dr Celia Pyper. Educated in the United States, she now lives in Bath.